Content

....

Leaving the wilderness...

It's been a hard year or so. Internationally, there's been COVID-19, wars, fires, suffering, persecution, political conflicts ... and for all of us, personally, there has been illness, missed opportunities and celebrations, separation from loved ones ... It has felt a bit like the 'wilderness years'. Yet, as our series in Numbers reminds us, our lives as God's people are about travelling *through* the wilderness, heading forwards to a good future.

Our Bible readings in this issue reflect the grand sweep of God's story: from God's people, wandering in the desert, to King David with his courageous following, disastrous failures, and faithful heart. Then, on to the long-awaited King Jesus whose journey here on earth may seem neither easy nor glorious. But as Tanya Ferdinandusz reminds us: '... he will *never* stop pleasing the Father. He *will* fulfil his mission.' And so, to his church. Esther Bailey leads us to Ephesus, where we find Timothy working hard to keep God's people faithful to him in a society that acclaims the greatness of other gods (sound familiar?).

In this wilderness world, we may sometimes feel lost 'in obscurity'. Remembering Jesus, his suffering and hope of eternity, Tanya's poem points us again to God's love and eternal purposes found in him: 'You are my Son, the Beloved; with you I am well pleased' (Luke 3:22, NRSV). In spite of our struggles, we too hear his whisper of love that encourages us to take up the opportunities of today, as we walk with Jesus towards his coming kingdom.

'Tricia and Emlyn Williams
Editors

Daily Bread toolbox

'Tricia & Emlyn Williams worked with Scripture Union for many years. Emlyn led Schools ministry, then worked with SU International. 'Tricia was also part of the Schools team and later worked for SU Publishing, developing, writing and editing Bible resources. Having completed research in the area of faith and dementia, she continues with writing and editing faith resources. Retired from his role as discipleship pastor in a local church, Emlyn now continues his writing and talking-with-people ministries.

WAY IN

This page introduces both the notes and the writer. It sets the scene and tells you what you need to know to get into each series.

A DAY'S NOTE

The notes for each day include five key elements: *Prepare, Read* (the Bible passage for the day), *Explore, Respond* and *Bible in a year.* These are intended to provide a helpful way of meeting God in his Word.

PREPARE

Prepare yourself to meet with God and pray that the Holy Spirit will help you to understand and respond to what you read.

READ

Read the Bible passage, taking time to absorb and simply enjoy it. A verse or two from the Bible text is usually included on each page, but it's important to read the whole passage.

EXPLORE

Explore the meaning of the passage, listening for what God may be saying to you. Before you read the comment, ask yourself: what is the main point of this passage? What is God showing me about himself or about my life? Is there a promise or a command, a warning or example to take special notice of?

RESPOND

Respond to what God has shown you in the passage in worship and pray for yourself and others. Decide how to share your discoveries with others.

BIBLE IN A YEAR

If your aim is to know God and his Word more deeply, why not follow this plan and read the whole Bible in one year?

Dr Luke has a story to tell. It's a super incredible,

Catching the Bible bug

Alison Pickering shares how Scripture Union's *Diary of a Disciple* is opening up the Bible and getting children to read it regularly – even those with no church background.

Alison works for outreach charity The Urban Family. For 15 years, she ran weekly clubs, partnering with four north-west London churches, with the aim of introducing non-church children to Jesus. She had also been using SU's *Diary of a Disciple: Luke's Story* in a discipleship group of three children with another church, and they loved it.

So, when the pandemic came and, with it, the first national lockdown, Alison decided to set up an online club to include the children without church backgrounds too, and use *Diary of a Disciple* as its basis.

'We got a copy of the book to each child. Originally, I'd planned to read a short extract to them each day, but they were so keen that things quickly evolved! So, from March to July 2020, we had a 45-minute afternoon slot, Monday to Friday, which we called *Live at Five*. We'd start with a prayer and a couple of worship songs, a game of some sort and then we would read a page or two of Luke's story from the

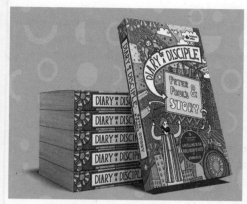

Diary of a Disciple books. Finally, I would give a short talk. Every Saturday, we'd have a session to review what we'd learned during the week.'

Children couldn't put *Diary of a Disciple* down

Most of the children never went to church and had never picked up a Bible before, let alone read one. 'They didn't know the Gospel of Luke at all,' Alison says. 'But at our online gatherings, the children were vying to get to read the next part of *Diary of a Disciple* out loud to the rest of the group.'

'Their parents were so grateful that we were encouraging their children's reading, because in many cases their reading levels had plummeted over lockdown. They were telling me how well written *Diary of a Disciple* was, how their child loved it so much that they couldn't put it down.

'Amelia was one of the few children in the group who was from a church family. Her mum told me how she'd tried for years to get Amelia to read the Bible regularly, to no avail. But now her daughter was telling her, "Mummy, I've got to spend time every day reading my Bible" – and off she would go! The children who weren't from church families were just as enthusiastic, telling me how they were sitting down and reading it cover to cover. Over the months, it became a habit for them – hopefully a habit that will last.'

Having finished Luke's story, the group started reading the next *Diary of a Disciple* book on the lives of Peter and Paul. Alison comments, 'I love these books. I've learned from reading them too, and I hope someday children will be able to read the whole Bible in this *Diary of a Disciple* format.'

Every child wanted to share and pray

Diary of a Disciple and the *Live at Five* online club have really helped Alison to engage with the children on unprecedented levels. She says, 'My personal experience of working with children over the past twenty years has been that if I ask someone to pray out loud, the room suddenly falls silent.

'Not any more! Increasingly, the children wanted to be able to pray for our protection and our needs, and to share what God was doing in their lives. Thursdays became

"Thoughtful Thursdays" – in the first 15 minutes of the session, children would take it in turns to share just one thing they were grateful to God for. Every child always had something to be grateful for, and all of them wanted to share.'

A doubling of numbers

The group of families grew quickly. On the first day in March 2020, there were 15 families, but three months later, 25 families were joining in, most on a daily basis. Alison comments, 'Going online opened up the freedom for children to invite cousins or friends. Some of them moved schools the following autumn and invited their new school friends.

'The group grew and grew. Now we have around 50 families in all – over a dozen of them from outside London! We just post a copy of *Diary of a Disciple* to them, it's easy enough to do.

'When the children returned to lessons in the classroom in September of 2020, we reduced *Live at Five* to one session a week. Nevertheless, most of the children still continue to come on the online sessions regularly.'

Now Ben just loves Jesus!

Alison recalls the spiritual journey of one young man in the online group. 'Ben who was ten had started coming to the kids' club we used to run before lockdown. His family weren't Christians and he'd never read a Bible in his life, he had no understanding of it. When we started up *Live at Five* on Zoom and reading *Diary of a Disciple*, he'd be there every day. And he loved it – he was the first child in our group to realise that what he was reading about in *Diary of a Disciple* was relevant to his own life today.

'Now Ben just loves Jesus! And he longs for his family to get to know Jesus too. When he came on our summer camp this year, Ben was asking us to pray for them.'

Holiday club will help children catch the Bible bug!

Now, Scripture Union has launched a new *Diary of a Disciple Holiday Club*, aimed particularly at children who don't have a church background.

Alison thinks it's a great idea. 'From my own experience, *Diary of a Disciple* really brings the Bible to life for children without church backgrounds. They love the stories, and it really helps them "get" who Jesus is. So, I hope and pray that it will help many more children like Ben to discover Jesus, to understand his message, and to follow him.' Find out more about the *Diary of a Disciple* holiday club resource at su.org.uk/diaryclub

A shorter version of this story first appeared in *Connecting You*, SU's free quarterly supporter magazine, in Winter 2021. If you'd like to receive copies of *Connecting You* and learn more of how God is moving in the hearts and lives of children and young people today, you can sign up online at su.org.uk/connectingyou.

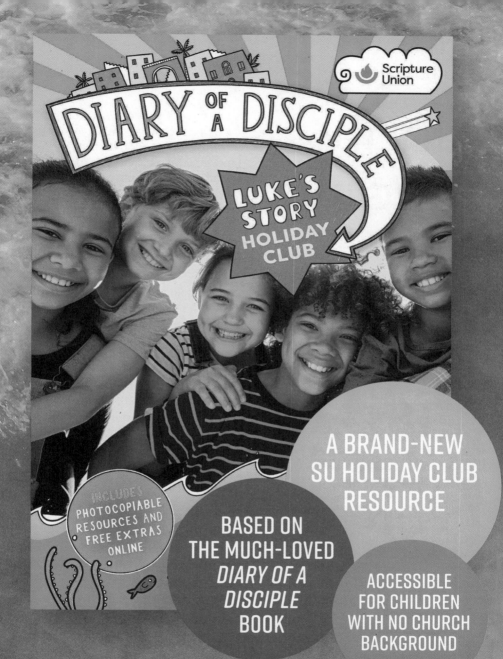

Get your leaders' guide and children's activity books at
su.org.uk/diaryclub

Kingly reading

The chapters we're going to read from 2 Samuel capture the tectonic plates of Israel and Judah shifting, seen in the power struggle between the 'house of Saul' and the 'house of David'. In just nine chapters, we encounter battles, grief and mourning, dishonour and unforgiveness, flawed human kings, judgment and retribution, the holiness of God and unexpected kindness lavished on a nobody.

We're going to see some wonderful qualities in King David, but we also know he's a deeply flawed, sinful man. Even in his best moments, David is only the faintest whisper of the greater King to come, Jesus: who lavishes kindness and unmerited grace, not on one individual but on all who call on his name; who doesn't build a temple but *is* the new temple through which we can meet with God; who doesn't seek to unify a nation but instead has won a people for God from every nation on the Earth.

How can we make the most of these chapters? First, let me suggest reading the verses carefully, really believing that God has meant each one to be there, even when they perplex us! Secondly, slow down (I hope I'm not writing that only for my own sake). My life all too often proceeds at breakneck speed, but if we quieten our busy hearts, we'll hear God speak through his Word. And thirdly, read prayerfully – talk to God about what you think and what you feel, and let his Word be a springboard into his presence.

About the writer
James Davies

James works for the Open University. He is married to Karen and they are part of a Newfrontiers church in Milton Keynes. They have three sons called Samuel, Benjamin and Joel, not much peace and quiet, and drink a lot of coffee.

Our vengeful hearts

PREPARE

Reflect for a moment on the wrath of God that Jesus absorbed on your behalf.

READ

2 Samuel 3:6–39

EXPLORE

What's the difference between just judgement and sinful revenge? David seemed to know it. After Joab's sneak attack on Abner (vs 23–27), David mourned for Abner with real tears (v 32) and wouldn't break his fast early even with the people's encouragement (v 35). In David's mind, this is clearly an incident of revenge for which God would hold Joab and his family line accountable (vs 28–30).

Joab had an all-consuming thirst for revenge for the death of his brother (vs 27,30). We'd have to be heartless to fail to understand this very human reaction. But what is the kind of heart response that God requires of us? God states clearly that 'Vengeance is mine' (Deuteronomy 32:35, NRSV), which Paul reaffirms to the New Testament believer in Romans 12:19. So the first thing we are to understand is that no matter the strength of our feelings and justness of our cause, we are not to avenge ourselves but to leave that responsibility wholly with God.

Now let's be practical for a moment. We probably don't face a situation anything like Joab's, but we do face betrayals, insults, loss and hurt. How are we to respond? Jesus shows us the better way: forgiving his enemies while trusting the goodness of his Father to judge justly (see Hebrews 10:12,13).

So Joab and Abishai his brother killed Abner, because he had put their brother Asahel to death ...

2 Samuel 3:30 (ESV)

RESPOND

Revenge is the desire to be God rather than to trust God. Is the Holy Spirit convicting you to forgive someone and to trust the Father?

Bible in a year: 2 Chronicles 33,34; Psalms 75,76

Saturday 2 July
2 Samuel 4:1–12

Hammer heads

PREPARE
Which of the fruits of the Spirit (Galatians 5:22,23) do you feel a particular need for at present?

READ
2 Samuel 4:1–12

EXPLORE

To Ish-Bosheth, Abner's death would have signified that the peace treaty (3:12–15) had failed – and his courage subsequently failed him (v 1). A leader without courage is like a drill without a bit or a mobile phone without a charge. Into this power vacuum, tread two captains, Baanah and Rekab (v 2), men of action lacking morality. Perhaps they thought they could take charge and unite Israel with Judah, plus gain a reward (v 8), but David has seen this story before (vs 9,10) and acts just as decisively (vs 11,12).

I'm reminded of these words: '…it is tempting, if the only tool you have is a hammer, to treat everything as if it were a nail' (Albert Maslow). Temptations for revenge, to use power (or violence in this case) to further our cause, are 'tools' or weapons we see in use throughout the world, from city streets to corporate boardrooms, to remote villages, to government reshuffles. These instincts, this sin, is in all of us. Jesus shows us a better way. To those of us who would lord it over others, he tells us to humble ourselves and serve (see John 13:1–16). To those of us who would seek power, he says, 'Pick up your cross because that's not the way my kingdom works' (see Matthew 16:24–28; John 18:36).

> When Ish-bosheth, Saul's son, heard that Abner had died at Hebron, his courage failed, and all Israel was dismayed.
>
> **2 Samuel 4:1 (ESV)**

RESPOND
What 'tool' has been in your hand recently? What 'tool' does Jesus want you to pick up and use? (See Ephesians 6:10–18.)

Bible in a year: 2 Chronicles 35,36; Luke 1:39–80

Control issues

PREPARE
Be still and know that God is in control and that he is good (see Psalm 46:10).

. . . .

READ
Psalm 52

EXPLORE
If the psalms are the Bible's hymn book, I'm not sure where today's psalm would fit in a modern worship service, with the 'tongue' that 'plots destruction', and practises 'deceit' (vs 2,4)!

This psalm represents an ancient wisdom that today's world would not recognise, but as Bob Dylan sang, 'You're gonna have to serve somebody.'* Even today with all of our scientific development, technology and education, it still comes down to the simple choice framed by this psalm: will we make God our stronghold or not (v 7)? At its heart, this choice is about control – seeking to gain control over our lives and our environment through prideful arrogance (v 1), asserting power through our words and speech (vs 2,4), lies that benefit us (v 3) and resources seemingly without end (v 7). But trusting these things means we are seeking refuge not in a place of safety but in our own destruction (vs 5–7).

God wants to rescue us from a miserable life of control-seeking to one of freedom and joy in which we trust the *one* who is in control (v 8). Our God is not a flash-in-the-pan remedy or a broken stick you lean on that pierces your hand; he provides safety for ever (v 8). Even when we have to wait for him and his answer, we know that he is good and to be trusted (v 9).

'I will wait for your name, for it is good, in the presence of the godly.'
Psalm 52:9 (ESV)

RESPOND
'Father, help me to put my trust in you alone today.'

*'Gotta Serve Somebody', Bob Dylan, Columbia Records, 1979.

. . . .

Bible in a year: Ezra 1,2; Luke 2

Monday 4 July
2 Samuel 5:1–25

God of the breakthrough

PREPARE
'Whom have I in heaven but you?' (Psalm 73:25). Thank God that you belong to him.

READ
2 Samuel 5:1–25

EXPLORE
Today's chapter gives us another stark contrast between the kingship of David and the kingship of Saul. We see David achieve the remarkable, but of course it's actually the Lord fighting on his behalf (v 10). The Jebusites in Jerusalem were a tough nut to crack. Joshua and the people of Israel had originally failed to conquer them when they swept every other tribe before them (see Joshua 15:63). Their past experience had made the Jebusites cocky (v 6), but David was having none of it and his men responded to his challenge, quickly taking the stronghold of Zion in response to David's request (vs 7,8). 'Then David knew that the LORD had established him as king over Israel and had exalted his kingdom for the sake of his people Israel' (v 12). Do you view the successes and 'wins' in your life as God's blessing?

Seeking to quickly snuff out the newly anointed king, the Philistines searched for David and their numbers spread out in the Valley of Rephaim (vs 17,18). But the Lord is the God of *hosts*, and numbers don't present a problem to him (vs 19,24). The name of that valley became known as 'Baal Perazim' (see NIV footnote to verse 20). The 'Lord who breaks through' (v 20, NLT) had rushed like a dam buster through the Philistines and left their false gods broken in the mud (v 21).

> The Jebusites said ... 'You will not get in here; even the blind and the lame can ward you off.' They thought, 'David cannot get in here.'
>
> **2 Samuel 5:6**

RESPOND
Are you facing an impossible challenge today? Take it to the Lord, the 'God of the breakthrough'.

Bible in a year: Ezra 3,4; Luke 3

Awesome God

PREPARE

Meditate on these words: 'Holy, holy, holy is the Lord Almighty; the whole earth is full of his glory' (Isaiah 6:3).

READ

2 Samuel 6:1–23

EXPLORE

We've just seen the Lord 'breaking through' against the Philistines in chapter 5, reducing them to rubble. Today, we see his power and judgement revealed in a different way. Reading about the Lord's anger towards Uzzah (vs 6,7) can be a real head-scratcher for us modern readers. Should Uzzah have just let the ark hit the mud?! But it was a major upset to David, too, who was both angry and afraid of the Lord (v 8). It reminds us that God is to be feared because he is holy – we can approach him only because Jesus has made it possible for us to do so.

David's joy is palpable when he brings the ark back to Jerusalem (v 14). What a wonderful example of abandoned, heart-felt, joy-charged worship (vs 14,16–19). And what a terribly sad story to see Michal, David's wife – underlined as the 'daughter of Saul' (v 20) – despise him for it. David returned home to bless his family (v 20), but Michal wouldn't receive it. Michal stands as a sober warning to all of us who at any time may despise the sincere worship of others. Though she was in close *proximity* to God's presence, her heart was far from the Living God.

> David was afraid of the Lord that day and said, 'How can the ark of the Lord ever come to me?'
>
> **2 Samuel 6:9**

RESPOND

Wherever you are, in whatever way you can, respond to God's holiness in worship.

Bible in a year: Ezra 5,6; Psalm 77

Grand design

PREPARE
'What is man that you are mindful of him ... the son of man that you care for him?' (Psalm 8:4, ESV).

. . . .

READ
2 Samuel 7:1–17

EXPLORE
When we first read this passage, we may think, 'Good for you, David! You're seeking to serve the Lord rather than enjoy your own comfort.' But the Lord doesn't quite see it that way...

God asks David a rhetorical question: 'Are you the one to build me a house to dwell in?' (v 5). In response, God answers his own question, 'I will make *you* a house' (see v 11, ESV). David had the resources to *build* a temporary temple. God promised to *make* David a wonderful everlasting 'house' that wouldn't perish or crumble (v 16). God had taken David from pasture to palace (v 8), had 'cut off' all his enemies and now promised to make David's name uniquely great (v 9). God also spoke of a time when he would bless David's heir who *would* build a temple (vs 13,14), and though he would discipline him for sin, he would not remove his love from him (vs 14,15). In time, the King of kings, Jesus, would be born through this blood-line.

God doesn't need anything from us. He is three-in-one, perfect, not lacking in any way. The fact that humans can serve him is because he chooses graciously to involve us and work in and through us, for his glory and our good.

'Moreover, the LORD declares to you that the LORD will make you a house.'
2 Samuel 7:11 (ESV)

RESPOND
How do you serve God? Have you slipped from joyful gratitude into somehow thinking that you're doing God a favour?

. . . .

Bible in a year: Ezra 7,8; Luke 4

Praying the promises

PREPARE
Thank God for his faithfulness to you.

- -

READ
2 Samuel 7:18–29

EXPLORE

Past, present, future: it's all here in David's prayer in a brilliant example to us of active, expectant faith. David looks back with gratitude for all God has done for him and for his people, Israel (vs 18,23,24). In humility, he is careful to acknowledge that it is God's greatness alone that has brought about Israel's success, from driving out the people ahead of them to rescuing them from Egypt (v 23). And this is interesting to me: David doesn't passively assume that God will continue to bless him or bless Israel and establish David's family line. Instead, David prays back to God the promises the Lord has spoken to him (vs 25–29), asking God to remember these words and to fulfil them. Off the cuff, how many promises from God's Word could you quickly recall?

I think David's prayer could be a key to our prayer lives today. Why not try this in your own prayer life? Write down in a diary or journal three or four promises from God's Word that impact you personally. Then make time as you pray regularly to bring these promises back to God, repeating to him what he has said in his Word, asking him to fulfil each promise, and for you to see the answers with your own eyes.

> Then King David went in and sat before the LORD and said, 'Who am I, O Lord GOD, and what is my house, that you have brought me thus far?'

2 Samuel 7:18 (ESV)

RESPOND
'For all the promises of God find their Yes in him. That is why it is through him that we utter our Amen to God for his glory' (2 Corinthians 1:20, ESV).

- -

Bible in a year: Ezra 9,10; Luke 5

Friday 8 July
2 Samuel 8:1–18

Floating branches

PREPARE
Thank God that you are loved: 'As the Father has loved me, so have I loved you' (John 15:9).

READ
2 Samuel 8:1–18

EXPLORE
In today's passage, we see David's amazing litany of successes (vs 1–5). Wherever David went, the Lord gave him victory (v 6). With such great success, came tributes from surrounding peoples, including from kings such as Tou (vs 9,10), and significant resources and wealth (vs 4,6–8,10,11).

What's the relationship between our actions and the Lord's? Verses 1 and 4 say David 'took' resources captive and verse 13 says 'David made a name for himself' (ESV). Yet verses 6 and 14 say the Lord gave David victory. Which is it? When God works in us and through us to achieve something for the kingdom, it can be all too easy for our unbidden thoughts to emphasise our role rather than God's. David was an incredible leader and king, yet he did seem to struggle with the sin problem of taking credit and receiving glory rather than giving it to God. Jesus once said that he was the vine and we are the branches, and without him we can do nothing (see John 15:5). This was true of David and it's true for us today. If you're ever tempted to glorify yourself rather than God, remind yourself that would be like rootless, floating branches, detached from a vine, trying to make grapes!

'The LORD gave David victory wherever he went.'

2 Samuel 8:14

RESPOND
Meditate on this verse: 'Abide in me, and I in you' (John 15:4, ESV). How can you abide in Jesus today?

Bible in a year: Nehemiah 1,2; Psalm 78:1–37

Loving kindness

PREPARE
Before you read further, list 12 ways in which God has been kind to you.

READ
2 Samuel 9:1–13

EXPLORE
Once again, we see in today's passage David's genuine honouring of Saul, actively seeking to bless anyone who's left in Saul's family line (v 1). Kings must be pretty busy, so for David to make time for this demonstrates what his heart was like. Mephibosheth must have been nervous (vs 6,7), yet David's intentions were wholly good (vs 9,10). This would come at quite a cost for David. I have three sons and they eat... a lot! Imagine how much food Ziba (Mephibosheth's servant) and his fifteen sons and twenty servants (v 10) could have powered through!

David wants to show 'God's kindness' (v 3) to Mephibosheth, Jonathan's son. Mephibosheth had no utility for King David – he was a forgotten nobody whose disability meant he couldn't fight in David's army or serve in his protection detail. The kindness David showed was one-way, unmerited and lavish –

Mephibosheth went from being in a place of desolate isolation to eating at the king's table (v 13).

In David's actions we see a foreshadowing of the loving kindness of Jesus – who sought out not just one long lost son, but came to redeem a whole people for God (see Titus 2:14). And who didn't only invite us to his table, but made a way for us to be adopted as children of God (1 John 3:1), and his banner spread over us is love (see Song of Solomon 2:4).

> The king asked, 'Is there no one still alive from the house of Saul to whom I can show God's kindness?'
>
> **2 Samuel 9:3**

RESPOND
Who can you show the kindness of God to today?

Bible in a year: Nehemiah 3,4; Luke 6

Sunday 10 July
Psalm 53

Foolish hearts

PREPARE
What can you thank God for today?

READ
Psalm 53

EXPLORE

I wonder at what point of his life David wrote this psalm. Perhaps in response to the foolish actions of people around him that we've seen through this series in 2 Samuel. Foolishness in the Old Testament doesn't signify a low IQ. It depicts the person who thinks they know better than God and deliberately chooses to ignore his ways. It can also describe the person who lies to themself about the reality of God – telling themself that he doesn't exist (v 1), though their conscience knows different.

Paul develops this theme in Romans and quotes today's psalm in Romans 3, emphasising that no one is righteous (v 1), no one has ever got it all together, no one ever has nor ever will be able to claim that they meet God's standards, God's law. Sometimes it seems people who do wrong in this life reap rewards, but God sees all (v 2), and it is a fearful thing to fall into the hands of the living God (compare Hebrews 10:31; v 5).

The bad news for me is that I'm foolish. I frequently think I know better than God, seen in my thoughts and actions. But thank God for the good news! That salvation *has* come 'out of Zion' (v 6). Jesus not only saves me but is to me the wisdom and the power of God (see 1 Corinthians 1:24).

> The fool says in his heart,
> 'There is no God.'
>
> **Psalm 53:1**

RESPOND
Thank Jesus once again that your salvation does not depend on *your* track record but on *his*.

Bible in a year: Nehemiah 5,6; Luke 7

'Oh, the places you'll go!'*

Oh, The Places You'll Go! is Dr. Seuss's wise and witty counsel to a young protagonist on the brink of great adventure. Optimism about what lies ahead is balanced by healthy doses of realism. The young adventurer will 'soar to high heights' but also experience 'bang-ups and hang-ups'. He will 'ride high' on waves of fame and popularity but also encounter danger, because 'enemies prowl' and 'Hakken-Kraks howl'! He will get 'mixed up with many strange birds'. The ride won't be easy but success is '98 and 3/4 per cent guaranteed'!

Jesus' baptism marks the beginning of his public ministry. After his 'graduation' ceremony at the Jordan, the Father publicly declares that he is 'well pleased' with his beloved Son (3:22). And I like to imagine that, as Jesus is sent on his way, the Father whispers in his ear, 'Kid, you'll move mountains!'

But Jesus' first stop is not a mountain-top but a desert, an initiation test of sorts from which he emerges triumphant (4:1–13). Then he's 'off to great places!' – mountains, plains, fields, lakes, synagogues, and homes throughout Galilee – preaching, teaching, healing, and exorcising. Jesus stirs up both amazement and controversy, love and hate, joyful acceptance and angry rejection. As he rubs shoulders with lepers and tax-collectors, he rubs the Pharisees up the wrong way. His popularity ratings soar... then plummet. But Jesus plods on. He will *never* stop pleasing the Father. He will fulfil his mission. Success is not just '98 and 3/4 per cent', but 100 per cent guaranteed!

About the writer
Tanya Ferdinandusz

Tanya and her husband Roshan have been married for over 25 years and have two adult sons, Daniel and Joshua. Tanya is both a freelance writer and freelance editor, and she has been writing Bible reading notes, articles and devotionals for over 20 years. She is the author of *Marriage Matters*, a book for Christian couples.

*Dr. Seuss, *Oh, The Places You'll Go!*, Random House, 1990.

Monday 11 July
Luke 3:1–20

Wilderness years

PREPARE
Meditate on what it means to be a person who is 'like a tree planted by streams of water, which yields its fruit in season and whose leaf does not wither' (Psalm 1:3).

READ
Luke 3:1–20

EXPLORE
Wonder and wonders surrounded John's birth: an angelic announcement, a sign, a miracle birth, an astounding prophecy. Everyone wondered, 'What then is this child going to be?' (Luke 1:66). But amid these great expectations, John retreats into the obscurity of the wilderness and remains there until the word of God calls him out of hibernation and thrusts him into the limelight (vs 1,2).

John's wilderness years remind me of the bamboo plant. After its seed is planted, months and years pass with no visible growth. Then, around the fifth year, life bursts forth from the ground and the bamboo plant reaches a staggering 80 feet in just six weeks! During those long months of invisibility, and apparent inactivity, a strong root system was being formed to support the giant plant that would emerge.

In the wilderness, the one who would prepare the way for the Lord was being prepared for his very public, very vocal ministry. When John finally speaks, it is like 'thunder in the desert!' (v 4, *The Message*). His words confront (vs 7–9), counsel (vs 10–14), comfort (vs 16,18), and convict (v 19).

> 'A voice of one calling in the wilderness, "Prepare the way for the Lord, make straight paths for him."'
>
> **Luke 3:4b**

RESPOND
'There is a time for everything, and a season for every activity...' (Ecclesiastes 3:1). Pray for God's wisdom to discern your season in life; grace, to navigate it; and strength, to be obedient to its demands.

Bible in a year: Nehemiah 7,8; Luke 8

Hidden years

PREPARE

'Take your everyday, ordinary life – your sleeping, eating, going-to-work, and walking-around life – and place it before God as an offering' (Romans 12:1, *The Message*).

. . . .

READ

Luke 3:21 – 4:13

EXPLORE

Jesus' public ministry is launched! Soon he will triumph over temptations, perform spectacular signs, and preach spell-binding sermons; ultimately, in submission to the Father's will, he will surrender his life on the cross. As Jesus himself put it, 'I always do what pleases him' (John 8:29).

But Jesus pleased the Father long before he was thrust into prominence. Even in obscurity, Jesus remained conscious of God's call on his life (Luke 2:41–50). His 'Father's business' was not just in the temple but, equally, in the ordinary, everyday struggles and challenges of family life, work life, and community life in an obscure little village called Nazareth. During those 'hidden years' between 12 and 30, 'Jesus grew in wisdom and stature, and in favour with God and man' (Luke 2:52). We *know* those hidden years were holy years because, although 'tempted in every way', Jesus didn't sin (Hebrews 4:15). Before Jesus even *begins* his public ministry, the Father publicly commends the private life of his beloved Son: 'with you I am well pleased' (v 22b).

Opportunity knocks ceaselessly through the everyday events and encounters of ordinary life, where most of us spend the greater part of our years. And as Mother Teresa often said – and demonstrated by her own life – we can 'do ordinary things with extraordinary love'.*

'You are my Son, whom I love; with you I am well pleased.'

Luke 3:22b

RESPOND

'Father, show me how to please you this week by doing ordinary things with extraordinary love.'

*www.motherteresa.org/her-own-words.html

. . . .

Bible in a year: Nehemiah 9,10; Psalm 78:38–72

Rave reviews to angry rants

PREPARE

Holy Spirit, help me to lay aside what I *want* to hear and open my heart to receive what *you* are saying today.

READ

Luke 4:14–30

EXPLORE

Jesus' public ministry began with a bang! The prophet of the year had vouched for him; divine favour crowned his inauguration (Luke 3:15,22); his Galilean ministry was a roaring success. By the time he returns to his hometown, Jesus is earning rave reviews (vs 14,15).

The carpenter's son is invited to take the pulpit, and both messenger and message are well received. When Jesus sits down, his audience is already hooked – all eyes are on him, and they are all ears as they wait for him to expound on the 'gracious words' he has proclaimed (vs 18–22). But although Jesus begins well, things don't end well.

When famous people make speeches, newspaper headlines and social media posts frequently highlight a few provocative phrases; and few bother to turn the page or click the link to find out what *more* was said or what was really said. Jesus leaves no margin for anyone to misinterpret his message. His 'gracious words' are not just for his Jewish audience; the good news of God's grace is equally for the despised Gentiles (vs 24–27). Tempers rise; and the fall in Jesus' popularity ratings is fast and furious! Rave reviews give way to angry rants, and Jesus not only loses his audience but is in danger of losing his life (vs 28,29)!

> He was teaching in their synagogues, and everyone praised him.
>
> **Luke 4:15**

RESPOND

Consciously or unconsciously, do I view some people as 'outsiders', who are beyond the reach of God's grace?

Bible in a year: Nehemiah 11,12; Luke 9

Happening words

PREPARE
Pray: 'Break open your words, let the light shine out, let ordinary people see the meaning' (Psalm 119:130, *The Message*).

READ
Luke 4:31–44

EXPLORE
Caesar Augustus' call for a census wasn't just an announcement; it was a proclamation that took effect and affected lives across the Roman Empire (Luke 2:1–3). Jesus' proclamation of good news effected the inauguration of *God's* kingdom (Luke 4:18,19). In the stories that follow, Luke shows how this proclamation of 'the year of the Lord's favour' is put into effect as Jesus brings healing and freedom from disease, demonic forces, and sin (vs 35,38–41; 5:20). These signs demonstrate that God's kingdom is breaking through the darkness, bringing light and life to people.

When God said, 'Let there be light', there *was* light (Genesis 1:3). The angel's declaration, 'I bring you good news that will cause great joy for all the people' (Luke 2:10), affirmed that God was delivering on his promise to bring deliverance. We speak today of 'happening places', where interesting or exciting action takes place. Jesus' words are 'happening words' – authority-backed, power-packed words that don't merely announce but *accomplish* that which they promise. No wonder the onlookers asked, 'What's going on here? Someone whose words make things happen?' (v 36, *The Message*).

> 'What's going on here? Someone whose words make things happen?'
>
> **Luke 4:36a (*The Message*)**

RESPOND
God declares, '...so is my word that goes out from my mouth: it will not return to me empty, but will accomplish what I desire and achieve the purpose for which I sent it' (Isaiah 55:11). Are you cooperating with God's purposes by sharing his life-giving Word?

Bible in a year: Nehemiah 13; Luke 10

Friday 15 July

Luke 5:1–11

Going deeper

PREPARE

'May I know thee more clearly, love thee more dearly, and follow thee more nearly, day by day' (Richard of Chichester).*

READ

Luke 5:1–11

EXPLORE

Jesus was no stranger to Simon. When Andrew introduced them, Jesus gave Simon a new name: *Cephas* or Peter (John 1:41,42). Simon had already answered the call to 'follow' Jesus (Mark 1:16–18) and experienced Jesus' power up close and personal when his own mother-in-law was healed (Luke 4:38,39). Simon accompanied Jesus as he preached the good news throughout Judea (Mark 1:35–39) and their base for this Galilean ministry was probably Simon's house in Capernaum.

Discipleship is a relationship in which Jesus keeps calling us to deeper levels of intimacy, trust, and commitment. But it seems that Simon is still splashing around in shallow waters! While Jesus teaches the crowds, Simon is busy with his nets (vs 1,2). Although he readily permits his boat to be used as a pulpit, when Jesus tells him to cast his nets in deep waters, Simon is sceptical. Despite saying 'Master', his obedience seems half-hearted (vs 4,5).

The breakthrough comes with a net-breaking catch of fish (v 6). It brings Simon to his knees. *Now* he addresses Jesus as 'Lord'. This glorious glimpse of who Jesus really is has Simon confessing that he 'can't handle this holiness', which exposes the depths of his own sinfulness (v 8, *The Message*; compare Isaiah 6:1–8). Simon Peter is finally going deeper (vs 10,11).

'Put out into deep water, and let down the nets for a catch.'

Luke 5:4b

RESPOND

'Spirit lead me where my trust is without borders.../Take me deeper than my feet could ever wander/And my faith will be made stronger.'**

*www.loyolapress.com/catholic-resources/prayer/traditional-catholic-prayers/saints-prayers/day-by-day-prayer-of-saint-richard-of-chichester/
**Hillsong, 'Oceans (Where feet may fail)'. See www.hillsong.com/lyrics/oceans-where-feet-may-fail/

Bible in a year: Esther 1–3; Psalm 79

He touched me!

PREPARE

'At the cross.../Where Your love ran red and my sin washed white.../I owe all to You Jesus.'*

....

READ
Luke 5:12–16

EXPLORE

Dr Paul Brand, a medical missionary in India, placed an arm around his young patient's shoulder. In halting Tamil, he explained that the progress of the leprosy could be stopped. He expected a smile, but the man started sobbing. Dr Brand asked his translator whether the man had misunderstood his explanation. After questioning the young man in Tamil, the translator revealed the reason for the tears – after so many years, someone had touched him.**

Jesus encounters a man 'covered with leprosy' (v 12), a disease that not only ravaged his body but made the man one of society's 'untouchables'. Leprosy sufferers had to leave their families and isolate themselves from the community. They faced loneliness, unemployment, poverty, and their 'uncleanness' even excluded them from worship. If they touched or were touched by someone, the other person also became unclean.

The law required that the person with leprosy shout, 'Unclean! Unclean!' But the unspoken cry of his heart was surely, 'Unloved! Unloved!'

Jesus grants the man's desperate plea to be made 'clean' (v 12b). 'Immediately the leprosy left him' (v 13b), a testimony to Jesus' great power. But even more poignant is the Lord's not-so-simple act of reaching out to touch him (v 13a). This touch – that would render Jesus 'unclean' under the law – foreshadowed the cross, where his 'love ran red' so that *our* sins would be 'washed white'.

Jesus reached out his hand and touched the man.

Luke 5:13

RESPOND

Who are the untouchable, the unpopular, and the unloved around you? How will you touch them?

*Chris Tomlin, 'At the Cross', 2014, www.azlyrics.com/lyrics/christomlin/atthecrossloveranred.html
**Story paraphrased from Paul Brand and Philip Yancey, *The Gift of Pain*, Zondervan, 1997.

....

Bible in a year: Esther 4,5; Luke 11

Sunday 17 July
Psalm 54

Perspective on problems

PREPARE
'Some trust in chariots and some in horses, but we trust in the name of the Lord our God' (Psalm 20:7).

READ
Psalm 54

EXPLORE
In a few days, we will read that the apostle Judas 'became a traitor' (Luke 6:16). Today's psalm emerges out of David's bitter experience of betrayal by his own people (see the superscription). The psalm has three sections: a plea for help (vs 1,2); seeing problems in perspective (vs 3–5); a promise of praise (vs 6,7).

David has confidence – both in God's power to save (v 1) and in God's readiness to listen to his prayer (v 2). Like the man with leprosy who prayed, 'Lord, if you are willing, you can make me clean' (Luke 5:12), David believes that God is both *able* and *willing* to help.

David not only brings his problems to God, he brings God's perspective to bear on his problems! Because of this, David doesn't merely see his enemies as 'arrogant' and 'ruthless' but, fundamentally, as 'people without regard for God' (v 3). In contrast, David has *great* regard for God. And his view of God is not dimmed or diminished by present trouble; instead, he looks to God as his mainstay and sustainer in the immediate crisis (v 4), and also as his ultimate vindicator (v 5; also v 1). It is his faith in this supreme 'triumph' that leads to David's promise of thank-offerings and praise (vs 6,7).

'Surely God is my help; the Lord is the one who sustains me.'

Psalm 54:4

RESPOND
In testing times, how faithful are you about reaffirming the truths you believe and exercising trust in the One in whom you believe?

Bible in a year: Esther 6,7; Luke 12

Remarkable things

PREPARE
What is the most 'remarkable' thing God has done in your life? Spend time pondering, marvelling, praising and giving thanks.

READ
Luke 5:17–26

EXPLORE
Many 'remarkable things' happened that day (v 26). The fact that Pharisees and teachers 'had come from every village of Galilee and from Judea and Jerusalem' (v 17) and that Jesus preached to a full house (v 19) suggests that remarkable stories about Jesus were already 'going viral'.

A group of men go to remarkable lengths to bring their needy friend to Jesus (vs 18,19). We sometimes speak of praise that *raises* the roof; here is faith that *removed* parts of the roof! Jesus acknowledges their remarkable faith and responds with a pronouncement that is both remarkable and controversial: 'Friend, your sins are forgiven' (v 20). With remarkable insight, Jesus recognises the silent storm of protest that is brewing (vs 21–23). As he looks at this man, who has been brought to him through a hole in the roof, Jesus sees beyond the obvious 'hole' in the

man's body to the void deep in his soul. Then he makes the man whole, body and soul. A remarkable claim about authority to forgive sins is backed by a remarkable sign (vs 24,25), the *visible* sign of physical healing validating the *invisible* spiritual healing.

'Remarkable things' are things worth remarking on! People are amazed and God is praised (v 26). Another story would soon 'go viral'!

They were filled with awe and said, 'We have seen remarkable things today.'
Luke 5:26b

RESPOND
What will *you* say, what will *you* do, to help the remarkable story of God's grace to 'go viral' today?

Bible in a year: Esther 8–10; Luke 13

Bread for beggars

PREPARE
'God is not a secret to be kept' (Matthew 5:14, *The Message*). Is your faith a well-kept secret or a secret widely shared?

READ
Luke 5:27–39

EXPLORE
'Evangelism is witness. It is one beggar telling another beggar where to get food.'* As a tax-collector, Levi was probably well off, financially. Socially, however, he was considered an outcast, despised as a traitor who collaborated with Rome. Spiritually, he was a 'beggar', a sinner in desperate need of God's mercy. When Levi encountered Jesus – 'the bread of life' (John 6:35) – he left behind his tax booth to follow him (vs 27,28). This beggar had discovered the life-giving bread that would satisfy his deepest hunger.

But when Levi abandoned that tax booth, he didn't cut ties with his buddies. His first action as a Jesus-follower was to host an open house for other 'beggars' like himself so that they, too, could meet the bread of life (v 29). Levi didn't argue or impose his views on his friends; he simply invited them to dinner and introduced them to Jesus.

The thought of 'witnessing' scares some of us witless! We may find it more comfortable and convenient to view evangelism as a task for missionaries or preachers rather than for us 'ordinary' Christians. But every Christian's testimony is both as simple and as urgent as one beggar pointing another beggar to the source of life-giving bread.

> 'I have not come to call the righteous, but sinners to repentance.'
> **Luke 5:32**

RESPOND
'Keep open house; be generous with your lives. By opening up to others, you'll prompt people to open up with God' (Matthew 5:16, *The Message*). In what ways are *you* doing this?

*DT Niles, *That They May Have Life*, Harper & Brothers, 1951.

Bible in a year: Job 1,2; Psalm 80

The case against Christ

PREPARE
'Open my eyes that I may see wonderful things in your law' (Psalm 119:18).

READ
Luke 6:1–11

EXPLORE
'Not every friend request is a friend request. Some are surveillance cameras.'* In Facebook jargon, Jesus had many 'friends' but some were really stalkers – the Pharisees and teachers who had 'come from every village of Galilee and from Judea and Jerusalem' (5:17). They went to the extent of following Jesus and his disciples to a dinner-party in a private home and criticising their friendships and dietary habits (5:29–30,33). They stalked Jesus out in the grainfields (v 1) and even in the synagogue (v 6). They watched closely, not to learn the truth but to build a case against Jesus (v 7).

Lee Strobel – confirmed atheist and journalist at the *Chicago Tribune* – set out to make a case against Christ. He interviewed many experts, seeking evidence against Christianity. Two years later, he weighed the evidence and found it so convincing that he became a Christian and wrote *The Case for Christ*!**

Unlike Strobel, the Pharisees failed to make the shift from scepticism to conviction, ignoring the logic of Jesus' reasoning (vs 3,4,9) and the compelling evidence of their own eyes (v 10). Although there are no further 'comments' on this particular thread, they banded together to build a case against Christ (v 11).

> But the Pharisees and the teachers of the law were furious and began to discuss with one another what they might do to Jesus.
>
> **Luke 6:11**

RESPOND
'Instead of facing the evidence and accepting it, you procrastinate with questions' (John 3:11, *The Message*). Pray for people with questions to start embracing God's answers.

*Source unknown.
**Lee Strobel, *The Case for Christ*, Zondervan, 2016.

Bible in a year: Job 3,4; Luke 14

Thursday 21 July
Luke 6:12–26

Important appointments

PREPARE
The first call of the apostles – even before being sent out – was to simply 'be with' Jesus (Mark 3:14). Spend unhurried time in prayer, and in reading and exploring God's Word today.

READ
Luke 6:12–26

EXPLORE
Luke records here two important 'appointments': Jesus' appointment with the Father, followed by his appointment of the apostles. When preparing for decisive moments and before making important decisions, Jesus spent extended time in prayer (see Luke 3:21; 4:1–2; 5:16). A whole night in prayer precedes the appointment of the twelve (vs 12–16) and is followed by an important address to the disciples (vs 20–26).

The word 'apostle' means 'sent'. The twelve, and later others from among the larger circle of disciples, would be sent out by Jesus on mission trips (Luke 9:1–6; 10:1–16). But since this sending would invite opposition and involve obstacles, Jesus often warned them about the cost of discipleship (9:23,24). The address that follows (the 'Sermon on the plain') is a reminder that kingdom people must learn to take a long view of life. Disciples are 'blessed' with promises of a kingdom and the kingdom blessings of deep contentment and joy (vs 20–23). Yet, while their appointment is a precious privilege, it is also one that brings problems and persecution (v 22).

John Stott described the Holy Spirit as one who 'before he is the comforter is the disturber'.* Disciples of Jesus must master the spiritual art of being comfortable with being *un*comfortable.

> Jesus went out to a mountainside to pray, and spent the night praying to God.
>
> **Luke 6:12**

RESPOND
Your daily appointment with God is an anointed time. Treasure it. Safeguard it.

*John Stott, *Sermon on the Mount*, Bible Speaks Today series, IVP, p 98.

Bible in a year: Job 5,6; Luke 15

Let love change everything

PREPARE

'Love, love changes everything/How you live and how you die.../Love will never ever let you be the same.'* How does God's love direct your living and shape your loving?

READ

Luke 6:27–42

EXPLORE

Jesus does not address everyone but only his disciples (6:20) – those 'who are listening' (v 27), presumably with a readiness to obey. Jesus tells his disciples how to respond to those who, by their hostility and hatred, make the demanding lifestyle of discipleship even more difficult. Instead of being reactive and retaliatory, which only perpetuates hate-cycles, his disciples must be proactive – accepting and absorbing pain, as Jesus himself did (Ephesians 2:14–16), in order to break vicious cycles and initiate life-giving love-cycles (vs 27–30). These are counter-cultural, counter-intuitive responses, making kingdom people distinctive (vs 32–35a).

Living and loving like this is costly and risky; 'love changes everything,' but also means that 'pain is deeper, than before'.* Living like this is an investment in 'treasures in heaven' (Matthew 6:20) and the rewards are out of this world!

As the song puts it, 'Love will turn your world around, and that world will last forever'!* The 'reward' Jesus promised is not an abundance of possessions, power, or positions but a growing relationship with and resemblance to our heavenly Father (vs 35,36).

'Live out this God-created identity the way our Father lives toward us, generously and graciously, even when we're at our worst.'

Luke 6:35 (*The Message*)

RESPOND

'As obedient children, let yourselves be pulled into a way of life shaped by God's life, a life energetic and blazing with holiness. God said, "I am holy; you be holy"' (1 Peter 1:14–16, *The Message*).

*www.genius.com/Andrew-lloyd-webber-love-changes-everything-lyrics

Bible in a year: Job 7,8; Psalms 81,82

Is the sermon done?

PREPARE

'Give me insight so I can do what you tell me – my whole life one long, obedient response' (Psalm 119:34, *The Message*).

READ

Luke 6:43–49

EXPLORE

The story has been told of a man who came late to church one Sunday. Slipping in at the back, he asked the usher, 'Is the sermon done?' She replied, 'No, the sermon was preached; it is yet to be done!'

As he concludes his Sermon on the plain, Jesus impresses on his listeners the importance of *doing* the sermon (v 46). The crowds had frequently marvelled at Jesus' sermons and signs (Luke 4:15,22,32,36; 5:26). But amazement isn't *action* and Jesus is preaching for a response: 'Work [my] words into your life' (v 48, *The Message*). This entails digging beneath the surface and never settling for the superficial: 'These words I speak to you are not mere additions to your life, homeowner improvements to your standard of living. They are foundation words...' (v 47, *The Message*). This is hard but necessary work for those seeking everlasting life.

Connected with this image of foundation words is the metaphor of the good tree (vs 43–45). As the builder must dig deep to reach bedrock, a tree must put down deep roots before it can yield good fruit. A faithful and fruitful connection to Jesus is one that allows his words to 'remain' in us, directing how we live and love (John 15:5–10).

'Why do you call me, "Lord, Lord," and do not do what I say?'

Luke 6:46

RESPOND

'You received Christ Jesus, the Master; now *live* him. You're deeply rooted in him. You're well constructed upon him ... Now do what you've been taught' (Colossians 2:6,7, *The Message*).

Bible in a year: Job 9,10; Luke 16

Praising God in the storm

PREPARE
What storms are you facing? What cares are weighing you down? Pour out your thoughts and feelings to God.

READ
Psalm 55

EXPLORE
David faces turbulent times (vs 3–5) because 'destructive forces are at work in the city' – 'violence', 'strife', 'malice', 'abuse', 'threats' and 'lies' (vs 9–11). Not only must he endure hostility and threats from enemies, his suffering is heightened by the pain of betrayal by a trusted friend (vs 12–14). The storms raging *around* David stir up deeply distressing storms *within*: he is 'distraught' (v 2b) and 'in anguish' (v 4); *The Message* version translates this, 'My insides are turned inside out' (v 4)! The horror of it all is overwhelming and David seems to be on the verge of a breakdown (v 5). Every instinct urges him to get away from it all, to 'fly away', to 'flee far away' from the turmoil (vs 6,7).

The turning point comes when David chooses to run *to* God instead of running *away*: 'I call to God' (v 16). Troubles do not disappear overnight. David confesses, 'Evening, morning and noon I cry out in distress' (v 17). The destruction of enemies is not a present reality but only a promise for the future, as implied by the repeated use of 'will' (vs 19b,23). But the storm *within* is stilled as David chooses to trust in God (v 23b) – the unchanging God who is 'enthroned' above every storm (v 19).

Cast your cares on the LORD and he will sustain you.

Psalm 55:22a

RESPOND
'And I'll praise you in this storm/And I will lift my hands/For you are who you are/No matter where I am.'*

*Casting Crowns, 'Praise You in this Storm', 2005.

Bible in a year: Job 11,12; Luke 17

In Obscurity

'You are my Son, the Beloved;
with you I am well pleased.'
(Luke 3:22, NRSV)

In obscurity,
I rediscover
my unfading identity:
'You are My child.'

Breathless,
my spirit breathes in
precious whispers:
You are treasured,
You are Mine,
You belong;
Believe it,
and be strong;
Beloved,
be loved.

In obscurity,
I am reminded,
Opportunity
still knocks.

I don't need fame,
a big name,
or people's acclaim;

I can please You
just as well,
(maybe more),
in humbler ways,
less visible ways,
everyday ways,
every day.

© Tanya Ferdinandusz,
March 2021

Jesus is Alive!

This Easter experience the amazing story of God's plan to save his people. Guardians of Ancora, developed by Scripture Union, is a free-to-download game that brings the stories of the Bible to life.

Experience the joy of knowing Jesus is alive and celebrate God's gift to all. Bring the story of the resurrection to life in the heart of a child this Easter. Download Guardians of Ancora for free and live the incredible adventures of Easter.

Download and play
Guardians of Ancora FOR FREE

Find out more at guardiansofancora.com

Scripture Union

Faith to follow Jesus!

The first half of the Gospel of Luke offers us a rich feast of stories about Jesus. He is in Galilee and has not yet started the long journey south toward Jerusalem. In these chapters, we have an extended season of preparation, not only for Jesus but also for his followers.

As we read through Luke 7–9, we need to be looking in two directions. First and most importantly, we will get to watch Jesus in action. What is he like, and what does he say? How does he act and react? How does he reveal his identity and his mission in these chapters?

Second, be sure to remain aware of the disciples. This diverse group of incredibly 'normal' men (plus women supporting him too, as we will see) are people very much in the process of learning. To be a disciple was to be an apprentice – someone learning on the job as they lived and worked alongside their master. They had a lot to learn, and they sometimes seem to miss the lesson in front of them. But let's not criticise them. Let's join them. We, too, are called to be Jesus' disciples: to be with him and learn from him. We will be glad of his patience with them once we recognise his need for patience with us too!

Let's pray that these days in Luke 7–9 will leave a mark on us as disciples of Jesus!

About the writer
Peter Mead

Peter is one of the pastors at Trinity Chippenham and a mentor with Cor Deo. He teaches at Union School of Theology and at the European Leadership Forum. He has written several books, including *Pleased to Dwell* and *Lost in Wonder* (both with Christian Focus). He is married to Melanie.

It takes one to know one

PREPARE

Who is the most influential person you have ever met? Perhaps a political figure, a military leader or even a powerful personality. Imagine how people felt when they encountered the authority of Jesus.

READ

Luke 7:1–10

EXPLORE

In this chapter, we see Jesus caring for outsiders. First comes a centurion. Actually, he does not come to Jesus. Jesus finished preaching and entered Capernaum. The centurion heard about Jesus and sent two delegations to ask for his help. The first group told Jesus how much the centurion loved the nation of Israel, provided for the town's synagogue and deserved Jesus' help.

If the first group built up the centurion, the second delegation offered a humbler, balancing perspective. This was the first encounter between Jesus and a Gentile in Luke's Gospel. And this Gentile knew that he was not worthy of being in Jesus' presence. He also knew that Jesus was a man of immense authority. Jesus could merely say the word, and his command would be fulfilled. It takes one to know one, and this military leader knew that Jesus had great authority!

Jesus was impressed by this faith. The man's servant was healed, but more than that, his faith in Jesus had proved to be an example to the Jewish people.

> When Jesus heard this, he was amazed ... and turning to the crowd ... he said, 'I tell you, I have not found such great faith even in Israel.'
>
> **Luke 7:9**

RESPOND

We know far better than the centurion did how much authority Jesus has. Dwell on his authority for a few moments and then pray for some situations weighing on your heart today.

Bible in a year: Job 13,14; Luke 18

Losing everything

PREPARE

Think of those you know who are suffering. Has your life experience prepared you to feel any of their pain and fear? Pray for them now.

READ

Luke 7:11–17

EXPLORE

Sometimes, the circumstances of others are almost too challenging. How can anyone understand the pain of this widow losing her only son in the ancient world? After showing his authority over disease for an outsider in the earlier verses of this chapter, now Jesus goes one better. In this passage, he shows his power over death. And he does this for a nobody. Obviously, this widow in Nain was *not* a nobody. But after previously losing her husband, now she had lost her only son. This tragedy meant that effectively she had no future: no support, no security and no family. Her prospects were bleak, but Jesus' heart went out to this poor woman.

The miracle Jesus performed in Nain was really a resuscitation from the dead. The boy was not resurrected, never to die again, as Jesus would be later on in Luke. He was brought back to life – a notable miracle, nonetheless. The crowd certainly noticed it. They declared that Jesus was a great prophet (v 16), and they saw in this miracle the evidence that God was at work in their midst. They spoke better than they knew, for God physically had come to help his people that day!

> When the Lord saw her, his heart went out to her...
>
> **Luke 7:13**

RESPOND

How does Jesus' power impress you in this story? How does his compassion for the widow stir *your* heart? Tell him – with words or even a song.

Bible in a year: Job 15–17; Psalms 83,84

So who is Jesus?

PREPARE

At a concert, a warm-up act sometimes prepares the audience for the real star. Imagine the excitement humanity should feel when the one sent to prepare for the Messiah steps aside!

READ

Luke 7:18–35

EXPLORE

Two of John the Baptist's disciples came to Jesus to confirm that he was, in fact, the Messiah. In the middle of the passage, Jesus gives his opinion of John. The final section offers Jesus' reflection on the people of his day. They wouldn't accept John, or Jesus, even though their styles were so different. Clearly, it was not possible to satisfy some people!

In this passage, the critical thing Luke highlights is the progression from the prophets of the Old Testament, to John (who was 'more than a prophet', v 26), to Jesus, who was the miracle-working Messiah. Jesus wanted John to know what he was doing for the blind, the lame, those with leprosy, the deaf, the dead and the poor (vs 21–23; see also Isaiah 61:1,2). John had come to prepare the way for the Lord, and now evidence showed that he was here.

John's role had been so significant. But do not miss verse 28. Even though John was greater than all who had come before him, even the least of us in the new kingdom is greater than John. If you have trusted Jesus, you are greater than John too!

> '...the blind receive sight, the lame walk, those who have leprosy are cleansed, the deaf hear, the dead are raised, and the good news is proclaimed to the poor.'
>
> **Luke 7:22**

RESPOND

Some people found any way they could to reject John and Jesus. Take a moment to tell Jesus that you accept him for who he really is!

Bible in a year: Job 18,19; Luke 19

Forgiven much, love much

PREPARE

Stories can be told to entertain or intrigue. Sometimes a story can 'undo' a person. Pray that God will give you a heart that is ready to be undone by Jesus' words today.

READ

Luke 7:36–50

EXPLORE

In this passage Jesus tells a little story which is within the larger gospel story about him. Jesus was at the home of a Pharisee (v 36). They were interrupted by a sinful woman who anointed Jesus with perfume. The Pharisee judged the woman (v 39), and so Jesus told a story – possibly the shortest story Jesus tells.

The story is about two men who owed money; both were forgiven (vs 41,42). That was it. But it was the follow-up question that did the work here. Which man loved the forgiving creditor more (v 42)? The answer was obvious: it was the one who had been forgiven the greater debt. So, Jesus drew out the parallels. The Pharisee's hospitality and kindness were limited. In contrast, the woman had been lavish in her devotion to Jesus (vs 44–47).

We celebrate that Jesus came to forgive sinners. But do we feel the personal power of that forgiveness in our own lives? The more we allow God to convict us of our sin, the more our hearts will swell with love for Jesus.

> '...I tell you, her many sins have been forgiven – as her great love has shown. But whoever has been forgiven little loves little.'
>
> **Luke 7:47**

RESPOND

Ask God to help you see your sin the way he sees it. Now, thank him for his forgiveness. Because of Jesus, we are fully forgiven – more than we often dare to dream. 'Go in peace' (v 50).

Bible in a year: Job 20,21; Luke 20

A good heart hears

PREPARE
Look at – or imagine! – a plant that is thriving. What makes plants grow well? What makes Christians flourish?

READ
Luke 8:1–15

EXPLORE
Luke begins by telling us about some women who were playing a vital role in the ministry of Jesus (vs 1–3). He goes on to relate one of Jesus' most famous parables. One farmer with one type of seed scattered it on four types of soil – with varying results. The story seemed simple, yet the meaning felt unclear. So the disciples asked him to explain (v 9).

Jesus pointed out how different soils gave different results. This is how it is with God's Word. Some people don't receive it because the enemy snatches it away (v 12). Others *seem* to receive it, but it does not take root (v 13). For others it is choked by the cares of this world (v 14).

Only one of the four soils produced a crop, 'the good soil'. Jesus said it represents those with 'a noble and good heart', those who hear, retain and persevere (v 15). It is challenging to realise that the state of our hearts is very important in how we receive God's Word. But notice the encouragement too: when we have hearts *ready* to receive from God, he can bring a hundred-fold crop!

'But the seed on good soil stands for those with a noble and good heart, who hear the word, retain it, and by persevering produce a crop.'
Luke 8:15

RESPOND
Praise God that we don't have to supply the seed, water or warmth. He can work wonders in our rocky hearts! Are we ready to hear?

Bible in a year: Job 22,23; Psalm 85

Saturday 30 July
Luke 8:16–21

Listen very carefully

PREPARE
If you want someone to really hear you, what do you do? Make eye contact? Give a strong, clear message? Repetition? What would God do if he wanted you to hear something important?

READ
Luke 8:16–21

EXPLORE
After teaching the parable of the soils, Jesus continues to restate a critical point from that story – 'Listen!' First, he uses the analogy of a lamp. Second, his family members become another way to repeat his point for those who were with him.

The purpose of a lamp is to shed light. There is no point in hiding a lamp. The radiance of the lamp is there to shine out and reveal what is there (v 16). By implication, Jesus' teaching is about light in a dark world. So, he says, 'consider carefully how you listen' (v 18; see also v 10). The light of Jesus' teaching brings with it a promise of judgment. Either we listen carefully and understand reality, or we don't listen carefully and slide further away from light and life and hope. There is no neutral option.

Then, we see his family were looking for him (vs 19–21). Jesus uses this to restate his point: 'hear God's word and put it into practice'. He seems to be taking every opportunity to underline something significant: listen carefully to what Jesus says!

'My mother and brothers are those who hear God's word and put it into practice.'
Luke 8:21

RESPOND
What would your life look like if you were listening carefully and responding appropriately to the words of Jesus? Pray that God will help you to do that today.

Bible in a year: Job 24–26; Luke 21

What can man do to me?

PREPARE

Ponder for a moment what makes you afraid. It could be a specific individual threat, or a global one. It could be one person or many. It could be a real threat or imagined. What makes you afraid?

READ

Psalm 56

EXPLORE

David was in a dangerous situation (see 1 Samuel 21:10–15). He had fled from threats in his homeland and had to pretend to be mad to survive in enemy territory. The threats were real, and the danger was significant. David was afraid. All he could do was cry out to God and pray for deliverance. In the first seven verses, David prays for God to destroy his enemies. After all, if the battle is between God and his enemies, his enemies had no hope of winning.

From verse 8 to the end, David reiterates the basic idea of the psalm. When he is afraid, he will trust in God. So, he calls on God to keep track of his tears and answer his prayer for deliverance (vs 8–11). He looks forward to praising God for the life he anticipates in answer to his prayer (vs 12,13).

When we put all the threats of evil humans on one side of the scale and God's care for us on the other, reality becomes clear. Humans are not more potent than our good God.

In God I trust and am not afraid. What can man do to me?

Psalm 56:11

RESPOND

It seems obvious, but it is the right way to respond. What makes you afraid? Pray to God. When we are afraid, let's continue to put our trust in God.

Bible in a year: Job 27,28; Luke 22

Monday 1 August
Luke 8:22–25

Who is this man?

READ
Luke 8:22–25

EXPLORE

Have you ever struggled to move from the classroom to real life? Perhaps a foreign language was easy with the teacher, but when you travelled to that country, it suddenly seemed so much harder. Sometimes Jesus takes us from the classroom to the laboratory of real life!

In the first part of this chapter, Luke had presented sayings of Jesus that point to the importance of listening to him. Now, he transitions into a sequence of events that will demonstrate his authority. This first event is recorded in brief, but leaves us with lingering questions.

It's a familiar story, briefly told. Jesus and the disciples are in a boat. There is a dangerous storm, but Jesus is asleep. They wake him in panic. Then Jesus stands, stops the storm, and questions their faith. After all his teaching about the importance of listening, perhaps Jesus expects them to have translated

hearing into faith. Maybe, as this section continues, what they see and hear will stir greater faith in them.

The response of the disciples is worth noting. Jesus asked, 'Where is your faith?' Their response? 'Who is this?' They see his authority over creation, and it stirs them to ponder his identity. As we continue through this section, let's be looking to see Jesus in action. We need to keep answering that same question: who is he?

> 'Where is your faith?' he asked his disciples.
>
> **Luke 8:25**

RESPOND
Who is Jesus? Pray for that question to linger in your heart in these days.

Have they 'herd' of Jesus?

PREPARE
As you think about your local area, what is the most obvious work of the enemy to bring harm and destruction? Can you list two or three things that come to mind?

READ
Luke 8:26–39

EXPLORE
When the forces of evil get hold of a life, the impact is genuinely destructive. As Jesus crossed the Sea of Galilee into Gentile territory, he encountered a man who had suffered significantly with many demons at work in him. The exorcism of these demons was a vivid demonstration of God's power as the demons went into a herd of pigs and immediately drowned them all (v 33).

Then we read of the reaction to the miracle (vs 34–39). The news quickly spread, and people came to see the radical transformation that had taken place. The change in the man was very significant and the crowd reacted with fear (v 37). They wanted Jesus to leave. As the story ends, we see Jesus sending the man back to his people to tell them what he had done for him (v 39).

In our culture, we may not typically see evil in such a tangible way.

Nevertheless, there are two big lessons for us to learn from this story: the forces of evil still seek to destroy lives in our world, and Jesus is still the only hope for anyone in this world.

> When those tending the pigs saw what had happened, they ran off and reported this in the town and countryside.
> **Luke 8:34**

RESPOND
In light of this story, pray for the enemy's work to be thwarted in your local area. Pray for Jesus' love for all people to be seen in a powerful way that gets everyone's attention!

Bible in a year: Job 31,32; Psalms 86,87

Wednesday 3 August
Luke 8:40–56

Interwoven grace

PREPARE
On a typical day, how many interruptions do you experience? Do you ever express your frustration to God? Does God sometimes interrupt your busy-ness?

READ
Luke 8:40–56

EXPLORE
This story weaves two incidents together. One interrupted the other. First, the only daughter of the synagogue leader was dying. Second, a ceremonially unclean woman was hunting for help. There was a twelve-year-old girl and a woman with a twelve-year-old problem. They could not have been more different. One was probably the princess of the village, while the other a bankrupt social outcast.

Notice how Jesus honoured the woman. He could have left her unnoticed and carried on to care for Jairus' daughter. Instead, he stopped and spoke with her (vs 47,48). If he had carried on, she would still have been healed, but she would not have been socially restored. See how Jesus called her 'daughter' and publicly acknowledged her faith. This was a beautiful moment, but it must have felt like a fateful delay for Jairus.

When news came that Jairus' daughter had died, everything seemed lost (v 49). Jesus was not perturbed. He took a small group into the house and raised her back to life! The interruption led to wholeness for the woman and a greater miracle for Jairus and his family.

> Hearing this, Jesus said to Jairus, 'Don't be afraid; just believe, and she will be healed.'
>
> **Luke 8:50**

RESPOND
Praise God that his grace pours out to rich and poor. Praise God that his grace pours out as *he* chooses, even if that sometimes interrupts our expectations and creates confusion for us.

Multiplying ministry

PREPARE
Do you sometimes feel discouraged about the impact that your life, or church, is having? If only Jesus could be doing the ministry in person, he would surely have a more significant impact! What is Jesus calling you to do?

READ
Luke 9:1–9

EXPLORE
The twelve disciples had been with Jesus, but now it was their time to be sent out by him. They got to do his ministry of making lives whole and pointing people to the purposes of God. There is a definite tone of humility in the instructions Jesus gave. They were to depend on God and live frugally (v 3). Perhaps their manner and their ministry were intended to reflect the character of God revealed in Jesus.

The disciples spread the word, and word certainly spread. In verses 7–9, we see that even the palace was stirred by what they heard. Herod, the regional royalty, heard about the ministry of the twelve. But notice: what was everyone talking about? Not the twelve, but Jesus. This is how good ministry works. As followers of Jesus represent Jesus in what they do and how they do it, society is moved to consider Jesus.

'Who is this Jesus?' This is the question that should be on everyone's lips!

> ... and he sent them out to proclaim the kingdom of God and to heal those who were ill.
>
> **Luke 9:2**

RESPOND
Pray for God to stir your motivation to represent Jesus in today's world. Pray that as you and others seek to do Jesus' work with Jesus' humility, the whole of society would be stirred to think about Jesus.

Bible in a year: Job 35,36; Philippians 1

Friday 5 August
Luke 9:10–17

A very practical school

PREPARE
What lessons is God teaching you at present?

....

READ
Luke 9:10–17

EXPLORE
As humans, we sometimes choose to learn something new. Perhaps we buy a book, or enrol in a class. And then, sometimes, Jesus decides to teach us during real life.

At the start of this chapter, the disciples had been out representing Jesus. Their impact spread extensively. Now there is more multiplication – this time the famous miracle of multiplication (vs 16,17). The disciples were ready for a rest, but instead, they found themselves before a vast crowd (five thousand men, plus women and children).

It is easy to focus on Jesus and try to imagine him doing the miracle. But Luke wants us to focus on the disciples and ponder what they were learning in this situation. They thought they knew best, asking Jesus to send the crowds away to get food (v 12). They did not realise it was time for a very practical lesson.

Jesus told *them* to feed the crowds (v 13). He made them count off the groups and have them sit down (vs 14,15). They were the ones distributing the food (and presumably having to answer questions about the source of the meal, v 16). And once it was all over, the disciples picked up 12 basketfuls of leftovers (v 17).

> They all ate and were satisfied, and the disciples picked up twelve basketfuls of broken pieces that were left over.
>
> **Luke 9:17**

RESPOND
Perhaps God will put you in the middle of a lesson when you are least expecting it. Pray that your heart will be responsive to what he wants to teach you, even as he uses you to bless others.

....

Bible in a year: Job 37,38; Psalm 88

Who do you say that I am?

PREPARE
Imagine standing among the disciples as you read these verses. What would *you* say?

READ
Luke 9:18–27

EXPLORE
Perhaps you sometimes struggle with anticipating a big event. Maybe you get over-excited about a holiday or overwhelmed with worry before seeing the dentist? Here, in this story, is a critical moment. Lots of people had different ideas about Jesus. But his focus was on his closest disciples. Who did they say he was? Peter gave the perfect answer: 'God's Messiah' (v 20).

As soon as the disciples recognise that Jesus is, in fact, God's chosen and anointed deliverer, he takes their training to another level. They had seen him teach, drive out demons and heal diseases. But they needed to know that the Messiah did not come just to do miracles. We cannot have Christ without the cross. So, Jesus explained what would happen to him (v 22). Then he laid out the implications for them as his followers (vs 23–26). To follow Jesus meant to take up a cross and walk in his footsteps. They would want to protect themselves, but he wanted them to live for eternity. Eternity was breaking into their world, and some would soon get a glorious glimpse of this (v 27).

We can understand the disciples struggling. We also struggle with what Jesus was saying. But notice – Jesus knew what was going to happen to him, and he didn't try to protect himself at all.

> 'But what about you?' he asked. 'Who do you say I am?' Peter answered, 'God's Messiah.'
> **Luke 9:20**

RESPOND
Ask God to grip your heart with the wonder of Christ's cross, and to keep your eyes on him as you live today.

Bible in a year: Job 39,40; Philippians 2

Sunday 7 August
Psalm 57

Praise because God wins!

PREPARE
Pray that God will give you a clear view of what causes anxiety and fear in your heart. Pray that he will provide you with an even more precise idea of his character, his loyal love and his glory.

READ
Psalm 57

EXPLORE
David was on the run from his enemies, hiding in a cave. In desperation he cried out to God for mercy and vindication (vs 1,2). In human terms, David was in real trouble. And yet, his psalm is filled with confidence. He is confident that God will hear his cry, thwart his enemies and deliver him. He does not simply expect personal deliverance. He looks forward to God's ultimate victory, where God's glory will fill the whole earth.

That description of ultimate hope in verse 5 is repeated at the end of the Psalm in verse 11. In the second section of the Psalm, he again presents the threatening activity of his enemies (v 6). And he expresses his confidence in God. This time he elaborates on his desire to worship and sing to God. It seems like his heart is overwhelmed by the great love of God, and his faithfulness that reaches all the way to the heavens.

A time of great danger brought the greatest of worship from David's heart. Why? Because God's goodness massively overwhelmed David's fear of his enemies.

> Be exalted, O God, above the heavens; let your glory be over all the earth.
>
> **Psalm 57:11**

RESPOND
'Father, do not let me dwell on things that make me afraid. Instead, help me to see your love and faithfulness so my heart will burst out in praise. Thank you that the ultimate victory will be yours.'

Bible in a year: Job 41,42; Philippians 3

Be confident: it is him!

PREPARE
Suppose Jesus is the Messiah from heaven, as Peter had declared. What would be the most significant confirmation of that fact? Open your heart as we read of this great endorsement of Jesus.

READ
Luke 9:28–36

EXPLORE
Peter had spoken up in front of the whole group of disciples and proclaimed that Jesus is God's Messiah (v 20). Then Jesus had started to tell them about his suffering and death. Who Jesus is matters more than anything else. So, in this unique moment, the three closest disciples get a most glorious glimpse and emphatic endorsement of who Jesus is.

They get to see Jesus in his heavenly glory (v 29). Then there are two – or three – witnesses: Moses, the founding figure of Israel, along with Elijah, the great end-times prophet of Israel. The third witness? As a glorious cloud engulfed them, they got to hear the voice of God the Father from heaven (v 35). As before, at the baptism of Jesus, the voice from heaven speaks of Jesus. This time it affirms that Jesus is God's chosen one (God's Messiah), who must be listened to (the prophet like Moses that was to come – see Deuteronomy 18:18).

This spectacular moment left a deep impression on those present. Peter refers to it years later in 2 Peter 1:16–21. They treasured the memory of it and lived their lives confident of Jesus' identity.

A voice came from the cloud, saying, 'This is my Son, whom I have chosen; listen to him.'

Luke 9:35

RESPOND
As you read of this fantastic moment, how does it reinforce your understanding of Jesus? How would your life be different if you were more confident in who Jesus is?

Bible in a year: Proverbs 1,2; Philippians 4

Down to earth with a bump

PREPARE
Do you ever get days when everything you do seems to be wrong? Ask God to help you if today is one of those days.

READ
Luke 9:37–50

EXPLORE
After the mountain-top transfiguration, everything seems to come back down to earth with a bump. We read of a child released from a demon (v 42), a prediction of Jesus' suffering (v 44), a child used as an object lesson (vs 46–48), and a brief report from a disciple (v 49). But in each of these stories the disciples are not doing so well.

The man with a demon-possessed child complains because the disciples could not drive out the demon. Then Jesus predicted his suffering again, but the disciples did not understand what he meant, and were afraid to ask. Next, we see the disciples arguing about who would be the greatest. Jesus pointed to their arrogant attitudes with the example of a little child. Finally, John reported that they had tried to stop someone from doing ministry because he was not one of the Twelve. Jesus corrected him.

Jesus is God's Messiah, but that does not mean his followers always get everything right. Because we are so slow to learn and live in such a broken world Jesus needed to come in the first place!

But they did not understand what this meant. It was hidden from them, so that they did not grasp it, and they were afraid to ask him about it.

Luke 9:45

RESPOND
Thank Jesus for understanding when you fall short, just like his original disciples did. We may be slow to learn and experts in messing things up. But Jesus is God's Messiah, and that makes all the difference!

Bible in a year: Proverbs 3,4; Psalm 89

Leaving the wilderness

If, like me, you are more attracted to literature than to algebra, you will not be instinctively drawn to a book called 'Numbers'. In the English Bible it has that name because of all the census data it contains. However, the Hebrew Bible calls it 'In the Wilderness', derived from the phrase in Numbers 1:1. It is really the story of the formation of the people of God in preparation to enter the good things he has in store for them.

We all find ourselves in the wilderness from time to time. Sometimes the Holy Spirit leads us into the wilderness, as he did Jesus, and the Desert Fathers in the fourth century. These intentional times of pressing into God, facing up to temptation and spiritual struggle can be so productive.

At other times, we find ourselves in the wilderness without any clear sense of purpose – dry seasons in our lives, when resources are scarce, and life is a struggle. The journey of God's people from captivity in Egypt to the Promised Land could have been as short as two weeks. Instead, it took 40 years. The physical journey was just the context for a deeper journey with God.

Numbers has three main sections and two 'transition' sections:

The wilderness of Sinai (chapters 1–10)

Travel (chapters 10–12)

The wilderness of Paran (chapters 13–19)

Travel (chapters 20,21)

The wilderness of Moab (chapters 22–36)

We are looking at the final travel section and the final period in the wilderness. There is a way out of the wilderness, but the lessons required can be tough!

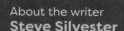

About the writer
Steve Silvester

Steve leads St Nic's, Nottingham, a city-centre church dedicated to growing disciples of Jesus. He also leads 'City Prayer', a movement uniting churches across the city.

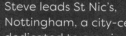

Am I trusting enough?

PREPARE

All true encounters with God begin with awareness of his holiness. This was the experience of Isaiah (Isaiah 6) and Peter (Luke 5). Take time to be still and recognise the holiness of God – his purity, glory and otherness.

READ

Numbers 20:1–13; 22–29

EXPLORE

You have to feel sorry for Moses. This chapter begins and ends with profound personal loss: the deaths of his sister Miriam (v 1) and his brother Aaron (v 29). Their prophetic and priestly gifts have been such a support to him as he has led his people. With Moses increasingly alone in leadership, the people focus their discontent on him for bringing them into 'this terrible place' (v 5).

At this time of intense pressure, Moses makes a mistake that leads to a third devastating loss: the opportunity to enter the Promised Land. In frustration he points to himself rather than God: 'Listen, you rebels, must *we* bring you water out of this rock?' In the crucial moment he did not trust God enough and thought it all depended on himself (v 12).

The secret to Moses' authority in leadership was always his humility (Numbers 12:3). This quality allowed God's power to work through him. Without it he was just a weary, ageing man.

For us too, in moments of pressure, it can be tempting to speak words that seem justified and feel good for a few minutes but lead to years of regret. At such times, I have to remind myself, 'It's not about me. Trust God. Honour him as holy.'

'Because you did not trust in me enough to honour me as holy … you will not bring this community into the land I will give them.'

Numbers 20:12

RESPOND

Where are your pressure points? Humbly bring them to God.

Bible in a year: Proverbs 5,6; Colossians 1

Facing up to failure

PREPARE

Psalm 19:12 asks, 'Forgive my hidden faults.' Are there things you prefer to hide that need to be brought to God today? Or things hidden from yourself that he needs to expose?

READ

Numbers 21:1–9

EXPLORE

We find it painful to re-visit our failures. We'd prefer to forget them and move on. But God's treatment of failure is more thorough.

The plague of snakes is a consequence of Israel's failure to trust God. This is expressed as impatience and grumbling (vs 4,5). When they do acknowledge their sin, they simply want God to get rid of the venomous creatures (v 7). But the snake that represents their failure is also the focus of God's healing and forgiveness (v 9). This may seem paradoxical: in order to be healed they have to look at the very thing that reminds them of their failure. God does not sweep sin under the carpet. He deals with it head on.

For us, the cross of Jesus represents both the deep shame of our failure and the means of our healing and forgiveness. As Jesus says to Nicodemus, 'Just as Moses lifted up the snake in the wilderness, so the Son of Man must be lifted up, that everyone who believes may have eternal life in him' (John 3:14).

> So Moses made a bronze snake and put it up on a pole. Then when anyone was bitten by a snake and looked at the bronze snake, they lived.

Numbers 21:9

RESPOND

Paul encourages us to 'consider … the kindness and sternness of God' (Romans 11:22). Is there a failure that you need to face up to? Facing it with God, despite the shame, leads to healing and forgiveness. You will discover both God's holiness and his grace.

Bible in a year: Proverbs 7,8; Colossians 2

Friday 12 August
Numbers 21:10–35

Vulnerable and violent

PREPARE
Use the words of Psalm 145:8–13 as a springboard for worship.

READ
Numbers 21:10–35

EXPLORE
Like the opening of yesterday's passage, this passage is uncomfortable reading. How can we reconcile a God who seems to command genocide with the God of love we know through Jesus? Taking the Bible as a whole, it is clear that both love and judgement are essential characteristics of God – there is more to these incidents than meets the eye. First, since the tribes that are 'completely destroyed' (v 3) emerge later in the narrative, it is clear that we should not take the phrase too literally. Secondly, God uses war in righteous judgement, even of his chosen people Israel.

I find it helpful to remember that, far from being an invading power, at this time Israel is a vulnerable group of nomadic refugees. Despite this, they are perceived as a threat and are refused safe passage through the territory of resident tribes (see also Edom's hostile reception, 20:14–21). Israel's unlikely victories make them seem more of a threat. This has the dual effect of stirring up more hatred *and* acting as a deterrent to those who would attack them. This is the story of countless minorities through history.

Jesus himself was perceived as a threat, both by Rome and by the Jewish authorities. The kingdom of God, ushered in through Israel and through Jesus, is an unstoppable force and always challenges vested interest (see Daniel 2:44).

> 'Do not be afraid of him, for I have delivered him into your hands, along with his whole army and his land.'
>
> **Numbers 21:34**

RESPOND
Who threatens me? Who perceives me as a threat? Pray for wisdom, protection and justice.

Bible in a year: Proverbs 9,10; Psalm 90

Unstoppable blessing

PREPARE

How do you feel about your life? Thank God for his care for you.

READ

Numbers 22:1–20

EXPLORE

For the third time on their journey from Egypt, the Israelites settle for an extended period, this time on the plains of Moab (v 1). From the hills above they appeared a huge, threatening group of people and animals, all requiring food and water (v 4). Their interaction with the king of Moab, Balak, and the pagan prophet Balaam takes three whole chapters.

Behind this story lies the foundational promise of God to Abraham: 'I will bless those who bless you, and whoever curses you I will curse; and all peoples on earth will be blessed through you' (Genesis 12:3). Balaam cannot curse the people whom God has blessed (v 12).

Later in our Scriptures, Paul wrestles with the 'irrevocable' call and blessing of God (Romans 9–11), and concludes that God's ways are inscrutable (Romans 11:33). For us, there is a two-fold application. On the one hand, we are all recipients of God's blessing. The blessings of Abraham reach all of us through Jesus (Romans 15:27). At the same time, God does seem to particularly bless some people, and this can arouse in us strong emotions, as it did in Cain (see Genesis 4:2–7) and Balak (vs 5,6).

> But God said to Balaam, 'Do not go with them. You must not put a curse on those people, because they are blessed.'
>
> **Numbers 22:12**

RESPOND

'Lord, I open my heart to receive all the blessing that you generously pour on me. Help me to rejoice when I see you blessing others. Keep me from envy, resentment, and the temptation to resist your will for them.'

Bible in a year: Proverbs 11,12; Colossians 3

Justice will triumph

PREPARE
On this day of reorientation ('the Lord's day', the day of resurrection), take some moments to review the past week and ask God to reset your compass as you spend time with him.

READ
Psalm 58

EXPLORE
When we look at our broken world, it's easy for us to lose hope, or for our hearts to become embittered (Psalm 73:2,3). This may particularly be so if you live in a country where the rule of law has broken down, and corruption is rife.

The psalmist describes a society like that (vs 1–5), but he does not fall into despair. Injustice is the fuel he needs for fervent prayer, crying out to God to intervene (vs 6–8). This psalm does express anger, but the prevailing tone is one of confidence in God's justice: evil will be punished, people guilty of abusing power will be held accountable, righteousness will be rewarded (vs 9–11).

The great Christian leader John Stott used to talk about 'double listening', with the Bible in one hand and today's newspaper in the other. Some of us listen only to our broken world and we are left with anxiety; some of us tend to listen to the Bible but ignore the world and become irrelevant to it. The psalmist's double listening enables him to address unjust rulers with prophetic courage (vs 1,2), God with honesty and faith (vs 6–8) and the faithful with hope (v 11).

> Then people will say, 'Surely the righteous still are rewarded; surely there is a God who judges the earth.'
>
> **Psalm 58:11**

RESPOND
Talk to God about how things are, how they should be, and how they will be because he judges the earth.

Bible in a year: Proverbs 13,14; Colossians 4

Attention, please!

PREPARE
'Lord, I still my heart in your presence. May other voices fade and yours become the one I hear. Speak, Lord. I am listening.'

READ
Numbers 22:21–41

EXPLORE
In this Shrek-like story, Balaam is travelling a narrow line – literally. On the one hand, he has permission to go to Balak if he does only what God tells him to do; on the other hand, God is angry that he is going in the first place. It is vital that he pays attention to God.

Through the donkey, God is turning up the volume: *do only what I tell you to do... Only speak what I tell you to speak.* Paying attention to God, the donkey becomes a prophet, oblivious to the messenger of God. The story enacts Psalm 32:8,9: 'I will instruct you and teach you in the way you should go; I will counsel you with my loving eye on you. Do not be like the horse or the mule, which ... must be controlled by bit and bridle or they will not come to you.'

How carefully do I attend to God? Do I recognise him guiding and directing me through circumstances? When I complain and become angry, is it because I have not recognised the 'angel of the Lord', God's messenger trying to point me in the right direction?

'... I can't say whatever I please. I must speak only what God puts in my mouth.'
Numbers 22:38

RESPOND
'Show me your ways, Lᴏʀᴅ, teach me your paths. Guide me in your truth and teach me, for you are God my Saviour, and my hope is in you all day long' (Psalm 25:4,5).

Bible in a year: Proverbs 15,16; 1 Thessalonians 1

Tuesday 16 August
Numbers 23:1–30

Irresistible blessing

PREPARE
Are you facing situations that cause you anxiety? Read John 1:5 and ask the Lord to give you his perspective.

READ
Numbers 23:1–30

EXPLORE

Balaam's stubborn insistence was corrected three times by his donkey. Now God uses him three times to resist Balak's stubborn intention to curse Israel. You might think that Balaam is a God-fearing pagan who comes under the direction of Yahweh and, like Cyrus for instance (Isaiah 44:28), fulfils his purposes. But later in Numbers, his sinister machinations are revealed and he is executed (Numbers 31:8,16). It is easy to forget that Balaam, for financial gain, is practising divination (22:7; 23:23), which God expressly forbids (eg Deuteronomy 18:10). Israel is called to be different from other nations (v 9).

Balaam was an imposing figure with a reputation of spiritual power. At times we can focus on the powers of darkness and feel overwhelmed. Individuals, power structures, or forces in society opposed to God can appear unstoppable. Why resist? How can God's purposes possibly prevail?

This story gives us a better perspective. Balaam ends up affirming the core elements of God's promise to Abraham (Genesis 12:1–7). Abraham will have many descendants (v 10); they will live under God's blessing (v 21); and they will occupy the Promised Land (24:5,6). God's blessing is irresistible.

> 'How can I curse those whom God has not cursed? How can I denounce those whom the LORD has not denounced?'
>
> **Numbers 23:8**

RESPOND
Have external threats caused you to lose confidence in God's blessings? Is it time to take hold of them again? God *will* complete what he has begun in you (Philippians 1:6). His blessings in Jesus still stand (Ephesians 1).

Bible in a year: Proverbs 17,18; Psalm 91

Seeing clearly

PREPARE

A prayer for today: 'Open my eyes that I may see wonderful things in your law' (Psalm 119:18).

READ

Numbers 24:1–25

EXPLORE

With his third attempt to make Balaam curse Israel, Balak gets more than he bargained for. Balaam moves beyond his normal psychic and occult practices, and he receives direct inspiration from the Spirit of God (vs 1,2). Speaking as 'one whose eye sees clearly,' he explicitly affirms the Abrahamic blessing (v 9, see Genesis 12:3).

In this oracle, Balaam looks ahead in the life of the nation of Israel. He sees them established in their promised land, led by great kings, with surrounding tribes subdued. Many of these prophecies were fulfilled under the early kings of Israel and Judah. For example, Agag (see v 7) was defeated by Saul, the first king of Israel (1 Samuel 15:8). However, under kings Saul, David and Solomon, Israel subdued the surrounding nations only temporarily.

It is not surprising, therefore, that both Jewish and Christian commentators have seen something more in these final prophecies of Balaam. As in much of the Old Testament, the vision of a future king points to a messiah. For example, the image of a future ruler as a star (v 17) is used of Jesus in Revelation 22:16. 'For no matter how many promises God has made, they are "Yes" in Christ' (2 Corinthians 1:20).

> 'I see him, but not now; I behold him, but not near. A star will come out of Jacob; a sceptre will rise out of Israel.'
>
> **Numbers 24:17**

RESPOND

Even Balaam realises that clear vision begins with submission to the Almighty (v 4). The fear of the Lord is the beginning of wisdom. What does this mean for you right now?

Bible in a year: Proverbs 19,20; 1 Thessalonians 2

Thursday 18 August
Numbers 25:1–18

Fierce holiness

PREPARE

'Let me tell you why you are here. You're here to be salt-seasoning that brings out the God-flavors of this earth. If you lose your saltiness, how will people taste godliness?' (Matthew 5:13, *The Message*).

READ
Numbers 25:1–18

EXPLORE

On the high places, Balaam has recognised that Israel is different from other nations (Numbers 23:9). They are called to be holy, as their God is holy (Leviticus 19:2). Meanwhile, on the plain below, they start behaving like the surrounding nations, lured into the sexual promiscuity associated with the worship of Baal, the fertility god. Their behaviour is reminiscent of that of an earlier generation, after receiving the Law at Mount Sinai (Exodus 32).

The blatant behaviour of Zimri (vs 6,14) epitomises the corruption of the whole nation, while the action of Phinehas conveys the holiness of God (v 11). This gory killing of a man and woman, possibly in the very act of sexual intercourse, sounds horrific. However, it served to protect the nation from the far more extensive punishment that God had pronounced (vs 4,11).

We may be more shocked by the actions of Phinehas than those of Zimri. The role of the priesthood was not just to perform sacred ceremonies: it was to maintain the holiness of the nation. Phinehas courageously acted as a true priest. Without holiness, Israel was just like any other nation. These stories have been preserved so that we don't make the same mistakes (1 Corinthians 10:6–8).

'...Since he was as zealous for my honour among them as I am, I did not put an end to them in my zeal.'

Numbers 25:11

RESPOND
Am I losing my Christian distinctiveness? Is there an area of compromise that needs to be checked?

Bible in a year: Proverbs 21,22; 1 Thessalonians 3

Women count!

PREPARE
'Defend my cause and redeem me' (Psalm 119:154).

READ
Numbers 27:1–11

EXPLORE

Thousands of years before the British constitution granted succession to the throne by the oldest heir, regardless of sex (2013), the daughters of Zelophehad raised a question of interest to many women. Normally, daughters received a generous dowry from their father, but the family land would be distributed among the sons. This would preserve the family name's deep connection with the promised land. But what if there were no male heirs?

I love these strong and intelligent women. Not only did they identify a legal loophole: they also anticipated their position when Israel came into the Promised Land (possibly anticipating that their tribe would be among the first to settle on the eastern side of the Jordan – see chapter 32). So their question, asked long before the land was conquered, arose from faith. God *would* fulfil his promises.

This passage shows us how laws which constitute so much of the first five books of the Bible were formed: a new situation arose for which there was no precedent, and Moses had to seek God's wisdom. The Bible does not answer all our questions. We also, collectively, need to seek God's wisdom, in line with what he has already revealed, when dealing with new situations. (Zelophehad's daughters' question raises further questions in the final chapter of Numbers.)

'Say to the Israelites: "If a man dies and leaves no son, give his inheritance to his daughter."'
Numbers 27:8

RESPOND
My future and security are not tied up with land, but with God himself. 'I say to myself, "The LORD is my portion; therefore I will wait for him"' (Lamentations 3:24).

Bible in a year: Proverbs 23,24; Psalms 92,93

Saturday 20 August
Numbers 27:12–23

After Moses

PREPARE
Do you need once again to 'return to the Shepherd and Overseer of your soul' (1 Peter 2:25)?

READ
Numbers 27:12–23

EXPLORE

Like many leaders, Moses was able to see further than his capacity to lead, and his earlier mistakes limited his ability to take people where he would have loved to have gone (see note for 10 August). Accepting this, Moses focuses on succession planning. So many of us fail to look beyond our own tenure. Great leaders develop others to follow after them. Joshua, Moses' successor, had been 'Moses' assistant since youth' (Numbers 11:28). He is 'a man in whom is the spirit' (v 18). This could mean that the Spirit of God is evident in him, or that he is a 'spiritual man', or that he has 'the spirit of leadership', as some translations put it. So Joshua's 'ordination' is an affirmation of what is already evident.

Moses has been anxious that the people would be left 'like sheep without a shepherd' (v 17). This phrase is deliberately echoed in the Gospels (Matthew 9:36; Mark 6:34). Jesus recognised the plight of the people of his day and stepped up to provide what they needed. I wonder whether the Gospel writers were wanting to convey that this 'Yeshua' is the one who can lead us out of the wilderness in a way that Moses (often equated with the Law) never could.

> So the LORD said to Moses, 'Take Joshua son of Nun, a man in whom is the spirit of leadership...'
>
> **Numbers 27:18**

RESPOND

You may not think of yourself as a leader, but we all have the opportunity to invest in others who will come after us. Is God calling you to be more intentional in developing someone else?

Bible in a year: Proverbs 25,26; 1 Thessalonians 4

Snarling dogs

PREPARE
'Search me, God, and know my heart; test me and know my anxious thoughts'
(Psalm 139:23).

READ
Psalm 59

EXPLORE
In July last year, a badly injured man was rescued from a remote mining camp in Alaska. A bear had attacked him and had returned every night for a week before he was eventually rescued. In this psalm the writer describes similar recurrent night terrors, like 'snarling dogs' returning at evening (vs 6,14). This is the experience today, for example, of victims of domestic abuse, and people living in areas blighted by anti-social behaviour or war.

For some of us, the 'snarling dogs' come in the form of crippling fear and anxiety, dark thoughts and intense loneliness. But, to answer the dogs, another refrain returns regularly and intentionally (vs 9,17). God is our strength and our fortress, our loving God (v 16).

This psalm contains a thought that is common in the Old Testament. Evil ultimately destroys itself. This is expressed as a prayer (vs 12,13), but it is just a question of time. Things that terrify me are laughable to God (v 8). The refrain reminds us, God is 'my fortress', my loving God. To this secure fortress we can go to watch for him to act (v 9), and to praise him (v 17).

But I will sing of your strength, in the morning I will sing of your love; for you are my fortress, my refuge in times of trouble.
Psalm 59:16

RESPOND
Whether the terrors we face are physical or psychological, the biggest battle is for the control of the mind. Can you identify your anxieties? Turn anxiety to prayer and choose to focus your mind on good things (Philippians 4:8).

Bible in a year: Proverbs 27,28; 1 Thessalonians 5

Monday 22 August
Numbers 28:16–31

Organised holiness

PREPARE

'Through Jesus, therefore, let us continually offer to God a sacrifice of praise – the fruit of lips that openly profess his name' (Hebrews 13:15).

READ

Numbers 28:16–31

EXPLORE

Unless we come from a culture that is familiar with animal sacrifice, chapters like this can seem very alien. Besides, we know that 'It is impossible for the blood of bulls and goats to take away sins' (Hebrews 10:4). What are we to make of all this? A helpful clue is found in Numbers 2. This details the formation of the tribes in their camps and journeys. They move in formation around the Tent of Meeting. Their whole life is to be organised around God's holy presence.

This chapter demonstrates amazing commitment, rigour, and discipline in Israel's approach to worship. It requires not only the sacrifice of animals but also of time. Israel's year is punctuated by special days like the Feast of Trumpets and the Day of Atonement, and special weeks such as the Feast of Tabernacles. These feasts, still celebrated by Jews today, require preparation and commitment. They are also times of great joy.

This makes me reflect on my own approach to worship. Am I too casual? Do I have a rhythm of prayer and worship through each week and through the year? When I go to church to worship, have I spent any time preparing myself? Do I actually need to become more organised around the holy presence of God?

'Be sure the animals are without defect.'

Numbers 28:31b

RESPOND

King David refused to offer to God something that cost him nothing (1 Chronicles 21:24). What about me?

Bible in a year: Proverbs 29,30; 2 Thessalonians 1

Moving in!

PREPARE

How does this time of prayer and meditation connect with the rest of my life?

READ

Numbers 29:1–11

EXPLORE

In the life of Israel, offerings and sacrifices were expressions of fellowship with God. There is particular provision for a sin offering in verse 5, and the Day of Atonement (vs 7–11) had special significance. But many of the offerings were for fellowship with God rather than atonement. In the wilderness, God's people were learning a discipline of fellowship with him. This gave their worshipping life a daily and yearly rhythm.

This life was not just for the wilderness. It was to be continued when they entered the Promised Land. Hence, the reference to grain offerings (v 3), which are only possible when a nation is settled, farming the land with regular harvests.

Many of us look back on wilderness times in our own lives as being particularly significant. These are the times of challenge, when we particularly draw close to God – we have no alternative. They are times when we are desperate for his voice, and when prayer and worship take a central place. But what happens when we move into ordinary life? Does all this take a back seat? Or do we learn to make the stuff of our settled lives (work, family, leisure) part of our worship?

'With the bull offer a grain offering of three-tenths of an ephah of the finest flour mixed with olive oil.'

Numbers 29:3

RESPOND

'Fill thou my life, O Lord my God,
In ev'ry part with praise,
That my whole being may proclaim
Thy being and thy ways.'
(Horatius Bonar, 1866)

Bible in a year: Proverbs 31; Psalm 94

Wednesday 24 August

Numbers 30:1–16

I wish I'd never said that!

PREPARE

Review your recent conversations. How do they measure up to Colossians 4:6?

READ

Numbers 30:1–16

EXPLORE

Women reading this passage might be outraged. In the context of the religions of the Ancient Near East, the Old Testament treats women with remarkable honour and dignity. Even so, a woman's role in the family was very different from most contemporary cultures.

In the Bible, vows are taken extremely seriously. 'When you make a vow to God, do not delay to fulfil it … It is better not to make a vow than to make one and not fulfil it' (Ecclesiastes 5:4,5). The Bible contains stories of men who make rash vows and have no one to get them out of the hole they have dug for themselves (eg Jephthah in Judges 11; King David in 1 Samuel 14). In today's passage, a father or husband is able to release a woman from a vow which proves to be 'rash' (v 6).

Maybe you have, from time to time, made a rash commitment. In such circumstances we need humility to accept our mistake, and the wise and loving counsel of friends or family to help us find a way to be released without devaluing the currency of our words. I wonder whether we tend towards the opposite danger: our words are so careless that vows become meaningless.

> These are the regulations the LORD gave Moses concerning relationships between a man and his wife, and between a father and his young daughter still living at home.
>
> **Numbers 30:16**

RESPOND

'All you need to say is simply "Yes," or "No"; anything beyond this comes from the evil one' (Matthew 5:37). 'Lord, may my words always be trustworthy and true.'

Bible in a year: Ecclesiastes 1–3; 2 Thessalonians 2

Uncomfortable reading

PREPARE
Before reading this chapter, remind yourself of the character of God through Psalm 103.

READ
Numbers 31:1–24

EXPLORE
This must be one of the most distasteful chapters of the Bible. It apparently condones genocide, including the destruction of children, and the distribution of women as commodities for men. If ever there was a chapter that needed to be read in the wider context of the whole Bible, this is it!

It could be argued that these gruesome actions were simply Moses' personal interpretation of the Lord's command to 'take vengeance on the Midianites', particularly as, under Balaam, their women had been responsible for leading Israelite men into idolatry (vs 15,16). However, it's uncomfortable reading.

Whether we acknowledge him or not, our modern reading of chapters like this is impacted by Jesus. Ancient history is littered with similar accounts of vengeance, devoid of any hint of embarrassment or shame, and the editors of Numbers seemed to find nothing in this chapter to object to. But in Jesus, a new way of thinking was introduced because he triumphed over 'the powers and authorities' *by the cross*, the epitome of shame and weakness (Colossians 2:15). This is why we find this chapter so difficult.

We may consider ourselves perfectly civilised and above the behaviour of the Israelites. But modern history shows that this is not the case. Every thought needs to be brought into subjection to Christ (2 Corinthians 10:5).

> The LORD said to Moses, 'Take vengeance on the Midianites for the Israelites.'
>
> **Numbers 31:1,2**

RESPOND
Do I consider myself morally superior to some people or cultures? (See 1 Corinthians 4:4.)

Bible in a year: Ecclesiastes 4,5; 2 Thessalonians 3

Friday 26 August
Numbers 32:1–27

Strength in solidarity

PREPARE
Read Philippians 2:3–5. How does this speak to you today?

READ
Numbers 32:1–27

EXPLORE

In my twenties, I led a mission team overseas. With a common purse, our only income was through the sale of Christian books. One of the team developed a romantic interest in a team-mate and began to build up a private fund to enable her to have treats. His actions, though reasonable to him, began to undermine the unity and morale of the team.

Moses faced a similar issue with the Reubenites and the Gadites. Their interest in land to the East of Jordan, outside of Canaan, was understandable, given its suitability for their flocks. But Moses angrily seized upon the implication: they could occupy *their* land and opt out of the fighting for the territories of the other tribes (v 6). An earlier episode in his people's history haunted him (vs 11,12). Without wholeheartedness, the mission to take the Promised Land could never be completed.

The two tribes were not faced with an either/or choice. Their negotiation with Moses allowed them to provide security for their families and animals before going on to fight.

In our lives, we may at times face an apparent conflict of loyalties. Our families and friendships, even our own personal ambitions, need to find their place in the context of bigger stories, nobler purposes, and collective visions.

'We will not return to our homes until each of the Israelites has received their inheritance.'

Numbers 32:18

RESPOND
Are you tempted to put your own interests, or those of people near to you, ahead of the collective need? Pray for wisdom to find a way forward.

Justice with safeguards

PREPARE
Regardless of the past and the future, it is only in the present that we can meet with God.

. . . .

READ
Numbers 35:6–34

EXPLORE
'Eye for eye, tooth for tooth' (Leviticus 24:20; Matthew 5:38) is often seen as a summary of Old Testament justice. Vengeance was actually the legal duty of the nearest male relative, making anyone who had accidentally killed someone else very vulnerable. In such circumstances there was the option of fleeing to a city of refuge, a place of protection and also of banishment (v 11).

This provision did not only protect individuals whose actions had led to someone's death. It also protected the land itself. 'Bloodshed pollutes the land and atonement cannot be made for the land on which blood has been shed, except by the blood of the one who shed it' (v 33).

Only the death of the high priest could release people guilty of manslaughter (vs 25,28,32), but in this case, it was a death by natural causes not sacrificial.

Hebrews 7:26,27 points out that Jesus is the High Priest whose death atones for all we have done (in the words of the old prayer) 'through negligence, through weakness, through our own deliberate fault' (*Book of Common Prayer*).

Everybody, at some time in their lives, wishes they could turn back the clock and undo a mistake. Even when we receive God's forgiveness, the consequences of our actions live on. 'The avenger' may not be a person, but a recurring thought.

'These six towns you give will be your cities of refuge.'
Numbers 35:13

RESPOND
Talk to God about any thoughts stirred by this reflection. You may like to use Psalm 32:7.

. . . .

Bible in a year: Ecclesiastes 8,9; 1 Timothy 1

To whom else can we go?

PREPARE
How honest are your prayers? Are there things you hold back from saying?

READ
Psalm 60

EXPLORE

Here's a paradox. On the one hand, being the people of God can bring desperate hardship; on the other hand, God is our only hope. When Jesus offered his disciples an opportunity to opt out, avoiding the challenges of discipleship, Peter replied, 'Lord, to whom shall we go? You have the words of eternal life' (John 6:68).

The situation in this psalm appears even more difficult: God has rejected his people (vs 1,10). And yet, God is sovereign (vs 6–8); their only hope lies in him (vs 9–12). This honest psalm helps the faith community to cling to the God who seems to reject them, confident of final victory (v 12).

We all face seasons in our lives where we struggle to see God working for our good. At times, as in this psalm, this is the aftermath of our sinfulness or rebellion. We are under God's judgement. The temptation may be to withdraw and hope the storm will blow over. But in the meantime, how can you live? As the 'prodigal son' found (Luke 15), the only sensible thing we can do is to set out in the direction of the one whose judgement we dread. Hosea expresses something similar: 'Come, let us return to the LORD. He has torn us to pieces but he will heal us; he has injured us but he will bind up our wounds' (Hosea 6:1).

> With God we shall gain the victory, and he will trample down our enemies.
>
> **Psalm 60:12**

RESPOND
This psalm was used 'for teaching' (see the introduction to the psalm). What is its lesson for you?

Bible in a year: Ecclesiastes 10,11; 1 Timothy 2

A story bigger than me

PREPARE
Is today just another day, or part of something bigger (see 1 Corinthians 2:9)?

READ
Numbers 36.1–13

EXPLORE

What a strange ending! An obscure legal ruling is hardly the resounding dénouement we might have hoped for. But maybe that is the point. When Zelophehad's daughters raised the question of their family inheritance, it took up only half of chapter 27. The rest was to do with Joshua succeeding Moses after his death. But we have heard nothing further about this. The story cannot end here – read on into Deuteronomy and Joshua to see how it concludes.

Today, marriage has become a public expression of a very private affair, 'our special day'. Marriage has also become an issue of individual human rights. This incident frames marriage very differently. The choice of marriage partner had huge implications for these women's family and tribe. Ultimately, their choice would impact on the fulfilment of God's promise in Genesis 17:8: 'The whole land of Canaan, where you now reside as a foreigner, I will give as an everlasting possession to you and your descendants after you; and I will be their God.' All the characters of this chapter are part of a story that is far bigger than them. 'My story' becomes significant when I learn to see it as part of God's story. If we don't, we may find ourselves back in the wilderness of self-preoccupation.

> 'No inheritance may pass from one tribe to another, for each Israelite tribe is to keep the land it inherits.'
>
> **Numbers 36:9**

RESPOND
Are we so preoccupied with our own story that we are preventing not only ourselves but others entering into the fulness of God's blessing? How does your story fit into God's story?

Bible in a year: Ecclesiastes 12; 1 Timothy 3

Old Testament narrative

What is Old Testament narrative and why is it there?

In a nutshell, narrative is story. And humans love stories! We become immersed in the events and invested in the characters. Think of the way people talk about fictional TV/radio dramas like *Friends*, *The Archers*, *Line of Duty*. Even journalists present their factual news reports as stories. From a jumble of events and opinions, they select and order their material to construct a clear story. If we are geared to respond to a well-constructed narrative, it is not surprising that God has chosen to reveal deep truths about himself and his purposes through narrative.

Well-told stories convey truth about the world and about our nature. A story gets past our defences, challenges our assumptions and leads us to a clearer understanding of the world and ourselves. 2 Samuel 12:1–14 is a great example of the power of a story.

The Old Testament writers, directed by the Holy Spirit, took the historical events of God's dealings with ordinary people in a particular nation and crafted them into narratives. These stories gradually reveal God's nature and his big plan to save and redeem the whole cosmos through Christ.

Why should we read Old Testament narratives?

Quite simply because God inspired these stories for our good, the New Testament urges us to do so (2 Timothy 3:16) and Jesus himself modelled how Old Testament narrative should shape our thinking. He used stories from the Old Testament to warn (Luke 17:26,28), to challenge assumptions and to make his listeners reflect more deeply on stories they thought they knew well (Luke 4:26, Luke 6:3).

Which books are in narrative form?

The main bulk of Old Testament narrative lies in the books of Genesis, Exodus, Numbers, Joshua, Judges, 1 and 2 Samuel, 1 and 2 Kings, Ezra and Nehemiah. However, there are also narrative passages in the books of the Prophets: Ezekiel, Daniel, Jeremiah, Jonah, Amos and

Hosea as well as a few passages in Leviticus and Deuteronomy.

Some helpful pointers for reading Old Testament narrative:

Get immersed in the story.

Old Testament stories are characteristically short on adjectives but long on action. The writers rarely describe or give direct judgement on the flawed and complex characters they present. So, the reader is left to evaluate the characters via their words and actions. If the writer has included a name or physical description, then take note and dig deeper! It is there for a reason.

Look out for where the action takes place. Settings in Bible narrative are loaded with spiritual meaning. Start to ask questions, for example, what happens when characters move eastwards? Why does Egypt crop up so frequently and what does Egypt represent? What is the significance of the wilderness/desert? And why does water feature in so many stories: from the Holy Spirit hovering over the waters in Genesis 1, to the wells of Abraham, the Red Sea, the Jordan, and the rivers of Babylon?

Look out for clues, shorthands, repetitions, contrasts, symbolic numbers. Ask yourself, why has the writer put this here?

Get to know how God's big story flows across chapters and books.

When you read or listen in big chunks you begin to see patterns, repeated words, phrases and themes. Think about what comes before, what comes after and where the narrative fits into God's big story. For example, David's fight with Goliath is not a stand-alone story. This short (but epic) event is part of a bigger story involving Saul's failure as Israel's king, David's journey to kingship and God's bigger plan to send his perfect and ultimate King, Jesus.

Finally, consider how the narrative contributes to God's salvation story or points forward to Jesus.

After Jesus' resurrection, Luke records two occasions when Jesus explained to his disciples how the Old Testament pointed to his suffering, resurrection and future plan for the world (Luke 24:25–27,44–49).

Writer Penny Boshoff

Penny spends half the year in Dubai with her husband, Andrew, where she teaches, writes and relishes sharing the good news with people from around the world. She currently serves as President for SU Council England and Wales.

Scripture Union

By purchasing *Daily Bread*, you are helping to support Scripture Union's mission with children and young people. Thank you!

Subscribe to our free supporter and prayer magazine at su.org.uk/ connectingyou

Pursue true godliness

Ephesus was a bustling cosmopolitan city, renowned for its wealth (it had the biggest bank outside of Rome), its culture (the temple of Artemis was one of the wonders of the ancient world) and its tolerance (all sorts of sexual behaviour were common and accepted). I wonder how that might compare with the society in which you live?

The church was being led astray by one set of leaders who had gone off on a tangent from the truth, and another set of leaders who were adding layers of additional requirements to the gospel. Paul needed to send someone to help the Ephesian Christians be confident in the truth. Paul's chosen envoy was a shy, insecure, comparatively young man with poor health – maybe not the most promising candidate on first appearance. But Timothy was loyal both to Paul and, more importantly, to God (Philippians 2:22), he was gifted (1 Timothy 4:14), and he knew the Scriptures (2 Timothy 3:15).

Paul is not able to write to the church leaders, as some of them were the ones who were leading the church astray. Although he directs this letter to Timothy, and includes many personal comments, he is also addressing the church at Ephesus as a whole, and through them, speaking to us today.

As you read, do you identify more with Timothy, thrust into a daunting role, Paul, a mentor and guide for younger believers, or the Ephesian church, needing encouragement and guidance to pursue true godliness?

About the writer
Esther Bailey

Esther lives with her husband John in north-east England, close to the Angel of the North. She is working with URC churches in Gateshead, Chester-le-Street and Stanley to engage with children and families not previously part of the church. Esther and John love exploring new areas in their aged campervan.

Loving correction

PREPARE
Can you think of a time when you had a difference of opinion with another church member? How did you deal with it? How was the matter resolved? (Or is it still ongoing?)

READ
1 Timothy 1:1–11

EXPLORE
'Timothy,' says Paul, 'I want you to command certain people not to teach false doctrines any longer!'

Reading this, I flinch – this sounds like a recipe for an explosive and confrontational church meeting, with both sides getting heated and entrenched. But Paul explains why he is opposed to these false doctrines – 'controversial speculations' distract people away from advancing God's kingdom (v 4). The desired outcome of Paul's command is love between all the believers.

Paul could have been self-righteous. He had warned the Ephesian church years previously to be on their guard against some of their own number distorting the truth and leading people astray (Acts 20:29–31). Instead, he puts in place a costly solution – sending his trusted companion to help the Ephesians get things back on track.

I wonder what Timothy felt, being sent on this mission? I wonder how he lovingly tackled those who were leading others astray? I wonder how he gently but firmly set out guidelines for authentic Christian living?

My goal in giving you this order is for love to flow from a pure heart, from a clear conscience, and from a sincere faith.

1 Timothy 1:5 (GW)

RESPOND
Jesus commanded us to love each other (John 13:34). How well do you keep this command? What would the church look like if every believer made this their priority?

Bible in a year: Song of Songs 1,2; Psalms 97,98

God's grace and mercy

PREPARE

How did you become a Christian? Was it a sudden turnaround, or has it been a more gradual process? Thank God for his abundant grace and mercy which have enabled you to know him and grow in him.

READ

1 Timothy 1:12–20

EXPLORE

Paul is able to be loving in his dealings with the church in Ephesus because he remembers where he has come from and what God has done for him. He describes himself as the least of the apostles (1 Corinthians 15:9), less than the least of all the Lord's people (Ephesians 3:8), and now as the worst of sinners (vs 15,16). How do you compare yourself to others?

As he gives his testimony in verses 12–17, Paul lists things he has received from the Lord – he's been given strength, considered trustworthy, appointed to God's service, shown mercy and treated with patience. Besides all that, grace, faith and love have been poured out on him abundantly!

As he considers the work God has done in his life, Paul praises God for six attributes – he is the King (of kings), eternal (who was and is and is to come), immortal (never going to die or decay, far greater than mortal humans), invisible (beyond the limits of our senses), the only God (unique), deserving of honour and glory!

> The grace of our Lord was poured out on me abundantly, along with the faith and love that are in Christ Jesus.
>
> **1 Timothy 1:14**

RESPOND

What has God done in your life? Spend some time praising him for all he is and all he has given you. Read Psalm 150, which praises God for just being God!

Bible in a year: Song of Songs 3,4; 1 Timothy 4

Pray for everyone

PREPARE

'As so often in the New Testament, the call to prayer is also the call to think: to think clearly about God and the world, and God's project for the whole human race' (Tom Wright).*

READ

1 Timothy 2:1–7

EXPLORE

Paul now turns to giving instructions about public worship, which he says should be of primary importance (v 1). Worship should not be insular, inward-looking and exclusive, but should reflect a concern for the whole community or society within which the church operates. Notice the number of times Paul says 'all' or 'everyone' in these verses – what does that tell us about God's concerns? And what does Paul say about the outcomes of prayer for leaders?

It might be easier to pray for those in authority if you live in a democratic, just society, but how do you pray for the leaders of a corrupt dictatorship? It is worth remembering that Paul's instructions here come at a time when Nero, who was famously cruel and hostile to Christians, was emperor. In the Old Testament, Jeremiah told the exiles to pray for the peace and prosperity of Babylon (Jeremiah 29:7). In Romans, Paul states that 'all authority comes from God, and those in positions of authority have been placed there by God' (Romans 13:1, NLT).

This is good, and pleases God our Saviour, who wants all people to be saved and to come to a knowledge of the truth.

1 Timothy 2:3,4

RESPOND

Who are the people in positions of authority in your community or country? Bring them before the Lord. Pray for wisdom, for personal well-being, and for decisions that encourage peaceful communities.

*Tom Wright, *Paul for Everyone: The Pastoral Letters*, SPCK, 2014.

Bible in a year: Song of Songs 5,6; 1 Timothy 5

Free to worship

PREPARE

'Faith in Christ Jesus is what makes each of you equal … whether you are … a man or a woman' (Galatians 3:28, CEV). Keep this verse in mind as you read today's passage.

READ

1 Timothy 2:8–15

EXPLORE

When we read the Bible, we need to be aware of the culture within which it was written. At first glance, Paul's views in this passage may seem to be misogynistic and sexist. But Paul was writing to Timothy (and the church) in Ephesus, a city dominated by the worship of a female god, Artemis, whose priests were all women. 'Christianity is different, everyone is of equal worth,' says Paul.

Both sexes are encouraged to break the stereotype – men should not be aggressive and argumentative, but should be devout pray-ers; women should not be slaves to fashion and image, but should be free to study and worship.

For many, the use of the word 'submission' (v 11) is emotive – but the passage does not state to whom it is that women should be submissive. Is Paul encouraging women to be submissive and obedient to God and his Word? Tom Wright, for example, translates verse 11 as 'They must study undisturbed, in full submission to God' (*Bible for Everyone*).

Eve was deceived, but she had not heard directly from God about *not* eating the fruit, whereas Adam deliberately disobeyed God's direct instruction to him (Genesis 2:17). Is Paul saying that women should study so that they will not teach error?

> Therefore I want the men everywhere to pray, lifting up holy hands without anger or disputing.
>
> **1 Timothy 2:8**

RESPOND

This passage is about allowing both sexes to worship freely. What things hinder you from doing so? Ask God to help you focus on him and worship without restraint.

Bible in a year: Song of Songs 7,8; Psalms 99–101

Qualities of a leader

PREPARE

My vicar's wife used to say frequently, 'You have the leaders you pray for!' She constantly challenged the church to pray for her husband and other leaders within the church. How often do you pray for your church leaders?

READ

1 Timothy 3:1–7

EXPLORE

As I write this note, the news outlets in the UK are full of the story of a government minister who has been found to be following a lifestyle at variance with the advice he has been giving the public. Suddenly, everything he has done in his role as minister, and the integrity of the government as a whole, has been brought into disrepute, and the minister has had to resign.

Within the church, we believe that everyone is acceptable, everyone can be forgiven, no matter what they have done but, says Paul, the behaviour of leaders matters! If the leader is shown to be acting without integrity, the whole church and God's name are brought into disrepute.

A person in a leadership role needs to demonstrate that God's transforming power has been at work in their public behaviour, their marital relationship, their character, their relationships to their family and to others outside the family, their ability to communicate God's word to others and their attitude to finance.

God sets high standards for his followers.

Here is a trustworthy saying: whoever aspires to be an overseer desires a noble task.

1 Timothy 3:1

RESPOND

Think of a Christian leader that you admire – what qualities, character traits or behavioural habits mark them out as a good leader? Thank God for them and pray that God would protect, equip and direct them.

Bible in a year: Isaiah 1,2; 1 Timothy 6

Getting God's perspective

PREPARE

Reflect on these words from the song 'Who am I?'*: 'You hear me when I'm calling / Lord, you catch me when I'm falling / And you've told me who I am / I am yours, I am yours...'

. . . .

READ

Psalm 61

EXPLORE

Psalm 61, like many Psalms, starts with a cry for help and finishes with praise. David is feeling so weak and unable to help himself – he prays for a solution that is far greater than anything he could do for himself (the rock that is higher than I, v 2). He has confidence in asking God for help because of his past experience of God's strength and protection (v 3).

Notice all the word pictures David draws of God in verses 2–4. Which of these brings you most comfort? During the Covid pandemic, when all our norms became like shifting sands, and life sometimes felt like wading through mud, I have been comforted by the numerous mentions of God the rock in the psalms.

As David turns to God and remembers what God has done for him in the past, he gains a more eternal perspective. The troubles he is facing are only temporary, but look at the glimpses of eternity in verses 4–8. Praise God that he also promises us the heritage of those who fear his name!

For you, God, have heard my vows; you have given me the heritage of those who fear your name.

Psalm 61:5

RESPOND

Try rewriting this psalm in your own words, putting in your own word pictures to describe God, your memories of his help in the past and your confidence in his promises for the future.

*Casting Crowns, Beach Street Records, 2003

. . . .

Bible in a year: Isaiah 3–5; 2 Timothy 1

Monday 5 September
1 Timothy 3:8–13

Serving well

PREPARE
Have you ever had to fulfil a menial role within the church, or in Christian ministry? How did you feel about it? What would you say were the qualifications for serving well?

READ
1 Timothy 3:8–13

EXPLORE

Deacons were appointed to fulfil practical roles within the church. Perhaps we would regard these positions as less spiritual, but Paul emphasises here that deacons must have an understanding of the deep truths of the faith (v 9). In Acts 6, where the first deacons were appointed to care for the practical needs of the church, the first qualification was that they were to be wise and full of the Holy Spirit (Acts 6:3).

Deacons, whether male or female, must be self-controlled in their behaviour and trustworthy in financial matters. They need to be above reproach in their behaviour and their relationships, especially with their family. In John 13, Jesus set an example of serving with an attitude of love for others.

The list of qualifications for a deacon matches that for leaders in verses 1–7, but Paul suggests two benefits of serving well (v 13) – they will earn respect (I wonder if that respect is from fellow believers, those outside the church, or from God himself?) and they will become more sure of their faith in Christ Jesus.

> Those who have served well earn the full respect of others. They also become more sure of their faith in Christ Jesus.
>
> **1 Timothy 3:13 (NIRV)**

RESPOND
Pray using the words of this song by Graham Kendrick:
'So let us learn how to serve,
And in our lives enthrone him;
Each other's needs to prefer,
For it is Christ we're serving.'*

* Graham Kendrick, 'The Servant King', Thankyou Music, 1983.

Bible in a year: Isaiah 6,7; 2 Timothy 2

Truth versus falsehood

PREPARE
Write a list of about ten words that describe what you think about the church. Are most of the words positive or negative, or are they a mix of both?

READ
1 Timothy 3:14 – 4:5

EXPLORE
Paul sets high value on the church (see Ephesians 3:10 and 5:25) and here lists three descriptions of it.

First, it is the household or family of God that puts us in relationship with all other Christians, with a concern to love them and a desire to see them reach their God-given potential. Second, it is the church of the Living God. The Ephesians were surrounded by temples and religious communities, but Christianity was unique in its worship of the living God, who promises that he is with us. And third, it is the pillar and foundation of truth.

A building needs a firm foundation so that it doesn't sink. It has pillars to raise the roof high to be noticed by all around. Paul recites a creed to remind the Ephesian church of the truth that is the basis of Christian belief – Jesus is both man and God; he is revealed to heavenly beings and humans, and is exalted on earth and in heaven (16b). Anything that leads people away from this truth is false.

In Ephesus (as in our world), there were many confusing voices (4:1–5). Perhaps remembering the shouts of the rioting Ephesians – 'Great is Artemis' (Acts 19:34) – Paul encourages God's people to guard the truth with focus on the Word and prayer (4:5).

> Beyond all question, the mystery from which true godliness springs is great...

1 Timothy 3:16

RESPOND
Reflect on each phrase of verse 16. How would you describe God's greatness?

Wednesday 7 September

1 Timothy 4:6–16

Being godly

Think about how you have grown and developed in your spiritual life. What things have you found helpful? What advice would you pass on to a younger Christian about becoming mature in Christ?

READ

1 Timothy 4:6–16

EXPLORE

In verse 2, Paul accused the false teachers of being hypocritical. Now, he advises Timothy to train himself to be godly and to set an example. What specific things does Paul encourage Timothy to do in order to keep this instruction (especially in verses 11–16)? Godliness – respect and reverence for God and reflecting God's image to the world – is not something easily come by. Note the use of the words train, labour, strive, devote, diligent, wholly, and persevere.

Paul emphasises the need for good teaching (vs 6,7,11,13). Studying the Word of God and teaching others what we have learnt from it will provide a firm foundation and will nourish the teacher and the hearers.

Three times in 1 Timothy, Paul says, 'This is a trustworthy saying.' He uses it to refer to Christ coming into the world to save sinners (1:15); to the aspiration to be a church leader (3:1); and here in verse 8, it refers to the idea that godliness has value for all things. What value do you place on developing godliness in your life?

> ... godliness has value for all things, holding promise for both the present life and the life to come.
>
> **1 Timothy 4:8b**

RESPOND

Psalm 119 is an acrostic poem in praise of God's Word. Use the words of verses 9–16 as a prayer, as you think about the role of studying God's Word as you train yourself to be godly.

Bible in a year: Isaiah 10–12; 2 Timothy 3

Dealing with need

PREPARE

Think about how your church identifies those in need – whether physical, emotional, spiritual, financial, social or any other type of need. How does it respond to these needs? What happens when need is great, but resources are limited?

READ

1 Timothy 5:1–16

EXPLORE

Timothy had been sent to Ephesus to confront wrong teaching, so whether he liked it or not, there was going to be conflict. Here, Paul gives him some guidance about how to speak to others, particularly those who were leading people astray. Following on from chapter 1 verse 5, Paul advises Timothy to treat others in the church as family members and to correct them lovingly.

Paul now turns his attention to those in need. Throughout the Bible, God shows his compassion to vulnerable people. Psalm 68:5 describes him as a 'defender of widows', so there is no suggestion that the church should economise by limiting the number of widows it supports. Rather, Paul is concerned that all of us take up our social responsibilities and help those within our circle who are in need, reflecting the nature of God in our daily lives.

Support for the vulnerable should not be patronising, belittling the recipient. Within Christian fellowship, everyone is worthy of respect and should be allowed to minister to others. What areas of ministry can widows, for example, be involved in (v 10)?

> Do not rebuke an older man harshly, but exhort him as if he were your father. Treat younger men as brothers, older women as mothers, and younger women as sisters...
>
> **1 Timothy 5:1,2**

RESPOND

How are you supporting the vulnerable? Maybe you are one of the vulnerable – does this passage give you ideas for how you can minister as well as receive?

Bible in a year: Isaiah 13,14; 2 Timothy 4

Friday 9 September
1 Timothy 5:17–25

Practical advice

PREPARE
Can you think of a time when you felt encouraged? What contributed to that feeling – a job well done, praise from others, seeing tangible results, financial reward, or a mixture of all of these?

READ
1 Timothy 5:17–25

EXPLORE
In these verses, Paul gives Timothy important pointers for dealing with church leaders.

First, *show appreciation*. The double honour referred to in verse 17 could mean appropriate financial renumeration, and affirmation or praise for things done well.

Treat them fairly. It is easy for a disgruntled church member to make an unfounded accusation, so Timothy is advised to only investigate misconduct if several people bear witness to it (v 19).

Be impartial. Don't prejudge someone on subjective terms, but equally, don't excuse someone because of your friendship with them (v 21).

Be cautious in appointing people to leadership (v 22). As in chapter 3, Timothy is encouraged to have a rigorous selection process. If a church appoints someone to leadership who then turns out to be unsuitable, the church bears the responsibility for their failings.

Be discerning. Don't judge by first appearances (vs 24,25). Find out what a person's character is like before appointing them to a leadership role (1 Samuel 16:7).

Some of these pointers were specific to certain situations, but some are always applicable.

> The elders who direct the affairs of the church well are worthy of double honour...
>
> **1 Timothy 5:17**

RESPOND
How could you show appreciation for your spiritual leaders to affirm and encourage them?

Bible in a year: Isaiah 15,16; Psalm 103

Money matters

PREPARE

Some believe that God blesses his followers with wealth; others, that Christians should give up material possessions. What place do you think that money should have in the life of a Christian? Thank God for his provision for you.

READ

1 Timothy 6:1–10

EXPLORE

'False teachers,' says Paul, 'are greedy, and see their ministry as an opportunity to exploit others for their own financial gain.' Christian leaders must learn contentment. This is a thought repeated in Philippians 4:11,12 and Hebrews 13:5. Paul is not saying here that Christians should aim to live in destitution, but he is saying that if our basic needs are met, we should be content with that (v 8).

Money in itself is not evil – Paul had stated earlier that everything God created is good, although it should be received with thanksgiving (4:4). Giving thanks reminds us that it is only through God's goodness to us that we have food, clothing, housing and money. Things go wrong when we allow money to become an idol and driving force in our lives, taking the place that God should have (vs 9,10).

Paul's words in verse 7 reflect Ecclesiastes 5:15 ('naked … as everyone comes, so they depart'). Jesus also warned against storing up treasure on earth, encouraging us rather to put our energy into generating treasure in heaven (Matthew 6:19). How might we do that?

> But godliness with contentment is great gain.
>
> **1 Timothy 6:6**

RESPOND

What would 'godliness with contentment' look like in your context? Read Agur's prayer in Proverbs 30:7–9 and put it into your own words to reflect your situation.

Bible in a year: Isaiah 17–20; Titus 1

Sunday 11 September
Psalm 62

My rock and my salvation

PREPARE

Think of a time when you were very conscious of God's help in a particular situation. How would you describe God's character and the help he gave in this instance? Thank him for his help.

READ
Psalm 62

EXPLORE

In this psalm, David seems to be having a conversation with himself. In the first paragraph he affirms his trust in God, reminding himself of God's strength and unchanging character. He is the source of David's salvation.

Then he looks at his situation, where people have proved unreliable and have deliberately tried to bring him to ruin. But, despite his hurt and his anger, David intentionally turns and puts his trust in God. Notice how many words and phrases are repeated in verses 1 to 2 and 5 to 8. In verses 1 to 2, David states his trust as a fact, but then he exhorts himself to trust.

David reminds himself that people who attack, hurt and upset others are only fleeting (v 9), but God is constant. He is always powerful and unfailingly loving. Power on its own could be frightening whereas love on its own could be weak. Praise God that he is both powerful and loving! Whatever circumstances we find ourselves in, these two qualities of God allow us to find peace as we commit ourselves to trusting him.

> Power belongs to you, God, and with you, Lord, is unfailing love.
>
> **Psalm 62:11,12**

RESPOND

Worship God for his power and his love – reread the psalm, pray, listen to worship songs that talk about God the rock, paint a picture, look at pictures of rock fortresses on the internet, climb a rocky outcrop...

Bible in a year: Isaiah 21,22; Titus 2

Summing up

PREPARE

'The fruit the Holy Spirit produces is love, joy and peace … being patient, kind and good … being faithful and gentle and having control of oneself' (Galatians 5:22,23 NIRV). Pray for more of this fruit in your life.

READ

1 Timothy 6:11–20

EXPLORE

As Paul reaches the end of his letter to Timothy, he sums up, and in doing so, repeats many of the things he has said previously. Look back at chapter 1 and note the similar words and phrases used.

Timothy is exhorted to fight for the faith – to be intentional about proclaiming the truth and pointing out false teaching. Evocative of the children's game 'tag', he is to run from falsehood, and run towards the fruit of the Spirit. He is to protect the truth (v 20) using the gift given him when he was ordained (4:14) and strengthened by the prophecies made concerning him (1:18).

And if this felt overwhelming, Paul reminds Timothy that he is doing it in the sight of God. Look at what Paul says about God in verses 13 to 16. God is vastly superior to anything else that people worship – the Roman Emperor who claimed to be a son of a god, Artemis the goddess, money, status or power. Paul's description evokes God's uniqueness, his greatness, his praiseworthiness. To him be honour and might for ever!

Fight the good fight of faith. Take hold of the eternal life to which you were called when you made your good confession in the presence of many witnesses.

1 Timothy 6:12

RESPOND

Paul finishes all his letters by saying, 'Grace be with you all.' What has been your experience of God's grace? Thank him that he gives grace so freely and generously.

Bible in a year: Isaiah 23,24; Titus 3

A mucky business*

'The Ideal World' is a UK-based TV shopping channel, broadcasting from studios in Peterborough. However idyllic that sounds to you(!), we simply don't live in an ideal world. It's complicated, at times brutal, confusing and distressing. Getting easy access to buying things doesn't quite address that!

2 Samuel 13–19 and accompanying psalms (63,64) face up to the real world. The moral dilemmas accompanying war are here, as are personal failure with its lasting impact, family feuding, misuse of power, sexual abuse and plots to overthrow the government. Amidst much mayhem, we are only given fleeting glimpses of God. That does not make us deists, believing that God the creator has a hands-off, non-interventionist approach to his creation. Rather, we see God working within the rawness of human sinfulness, using flawed people but remaining true to his promises. When David sins catastrophically, the birth of Solomon becomes a sign of hope. When Absalom has a cast-iron plan to destroy David, God ensures it is scuppered. We see God raising up people of faithfulness (like Uriah, Nathan, an unnamed woman, Barzillai) and giving hints of his kindness through David's acts. We gain fresh insight of God at work in the muddles of our existence and renew our trust that just as all this was background to the coming Messiah, so we are sure his promise of a new heaven and new earth will bring the ideal world (with no shopping!).

About the writer
Andy Bathgate

Andy retired from his role as CEO of SU Scotland in March 2020 after 18 years. He is married to Alyson and lives in Edinburgh, where they are both involved in the leadership of their local church. They enjoy visiting art galleries, reading all kinds of books and looking after their three grandsons.

*The title of MP Tim Farron's podcast on Premier Radio.

From indignity to victory

PREPARE

Ponder some of the ways in which God has been kind to you and then give him thanks.

READ

2 Samuel 10:1–19

EXPLORE

Conflict is easily ignited. David has good intentions in offering a peace agreement to the newly enthroned Ammonite king, Hanun. But rather than embrace peace, the Ammonites are spooked through suspicion or cynicism and humiliate David's envoys, cutting off half their beards and inflicting 'forced indecent exposure',* to put it politely! Hanun's father had been an ally of David when David was being harried by Saul. David now extends a kind hand of friendship only to have it bitten as if by a cornered dog. The kindness of God through his people can be misinterpreted, being perceived as a sign of weakness or raising suspicions of an ulterior motive. Kindnesses do not necessarily produce gratitude.

Conflict comes easily but is costly. Peace was in the Ammonites' grasp, but full-scale war ensues. They and their allies are crushed at the price of many lives. David's armies implement a strategy involving both military guile *and* trust in God. Trust in God does not breed complacency or a simplistic 'God is on our side' mentality. They devise strategies knowing that the outcome lies in God's hands and in his mysterious purposes. God gives the victory; Israel secures its territory and David is honoured. But a shock wave is about to hit. There is victory but also fragility.

'Be strong, and let us fight bravely for our people and the cities of our God. The LORD will do what is good in his sight.'

2 Samuel 10:12

RESPOND

Paul urges believers 'not to receive God's grace in vain' (2 Corinthians 6:1). What are the main threats we face as receivers of God's grace?

*AA Anderson, *Word Biblical Commentary: 2 Samuel*, Nelson, 1989, p147.

Bible in a year: Isaiah 25,26; Psalm 104

2 Samuel 11:1–27

From victory to indignity

PREPARE

O loving wisdom of our God / When all was sin and shame / a second Adam to the fight and to the rescue came.* Praise God for our rescue.

READ
2 Samuel 11:1–27

EXPLORE

Just because you can do a thing doesn't mean you should. David's growth in power means there is no one to challenge his actions. His control allows him to take whatever he likes, to scheme and to conclude with a shrug: 'forget it, it's not a problem' (v 25). There are too many similar stories of abuse of power by Christian leaders, bringing ignominy on Christ's church, trashing their own reputations and more importantly ruining the lives of victims. The ramifications are huge; one commentator drew a comparison between the consequences of David's sin and that of Adam and Eve's.**

This is atrocious behaviour for anyone, but for God's anointed king, the one intended to be the guardian of the people's rights and justice, it is catastrophic. He tumbles rapidly from all-conquering hero (chapter 10) to the curse of chapter 12 (vs 10,11).

The sole contrast to David is faithful Uriah the Hittite, who refuses to bend to David's tempting offers. Like the centurion applauded by Jesus for his faith (Matthew 8:5–13; Luke 7:1–10), this outsider stands as a rebuke to creeping complacency. The Lord is not happy with David. But as with Jonah and Peter and Thomas and with us, although there are inevitable and sad consequences of sin, God continues to work even with displeasing people.

Sin wants to destroy you, but don't let it!

Genesis 4:7b (CEV)

RESPOND

In what ways are you like David and in what ways like Uriah?

*'Praise to the Holiest in the Height', John Henry Newman (1865).
**Walter Brueggemann, *First and Second Samuel*, John Knox Press, 1990, p272.

Bible in a year: Isaiah 27,28; Philemon 1

Not a leg to stand on

PREPARE

Sin is horrible but not lethal for those in Christ. Come to him, knowing that 'grace upon grace' is available to you (John 1:16, RSV).

READ

2 Samuel 12:1–14

EXPLORE

Why is it so much easier to angrily condemn others' sins than to recognise our own? Did David think he'd got away with adultery and murder and hoped it would never surface? Or had it simply not dawned on him how gravely he had offended God? Whatever, he had somehow blanked his mind of guilt. But he is quick to boil over when he encounters the self-centred rich man, abusing power to crush a poor family.

Most lacked the courage to call David out. Nathan, a true prophet, refuses the 'yes-man' role. Speaking truth to power demands huge courage and great wisdom. Nathan's parable evokes a self-righteous reaction that demands an over-the-top penalty (v 5). Nathan makes the link explicit (v 7) and David gets it. He could have remained in control, silencing Nathan and burying the whole sorry episode. But he is immediately repentant. David is a sinner but one who listens to God's voice, who in his heart of hearts loves God and wants to please him. There will be sad consequences of his sin; 'a long destiny of sword-shaped life';* but God remains true to his promise (see 2 Samuel 7:4–17). All this is the prelude to a series of tragic but not pointless events. They will still lead somewhere in God's purpose.

Have mercy on me, O God, according to your unfailing love; according to your great compassion blot out my transgressions.

Psalm 51:1

RESPOND

How do we ensure our hidden sins do not compromise our relationship with God? Who keeps us accountable?

*Brueggemann, p281.

Bible in a year: Isaiah 29,30; Hebrews 1

Sons, sin and assurance

PREPARE
What's on your heart as you come to God? He wants to listen, even to hear you 'spill out ... complaints before him' (Psalm 142:2, *The Message*).

READ
2 Samuel 12:15–31

EXPLORE
When Jesus stood amongst the weeping mourners at Lazarus' grave, 'a deep anger welled up within him' (John 11:33, NLT). It was a severe response to the chaos caused by sin in God's good creation. Sin shatters everything it touches, bringing sadness and confusion across generations. The death of a child intensifies our agony as we ask, 'why?'

The deadly illness that strikes David and Uriah's wife's (a reminder of the adultery) son is heart-rending and raises numerous questions. It troubles us, making us contemplate the mysterious ways of God and the horrific impact of human behaviour on those who are blameless. In other places David teaches us how to lament when faced with such confusion (eg Psalm 13; 42; 43; 63; 64; 142).

But here, David's reaction is perplexing. Pleading with God is understandable but his sudden return to normal seems uncaring and is no way a model for our behaviour. No easy answers are provided. We note that we cannot dictate to others how long their mourning should last. Secondly, the thrust of this narrative is about looking forward. Amid disaster another son is born. The line continues and Solomon becomes the sign that God's promise is intact. As believers in the King who has come in this royal line, we stand as the beneficiaries of this history.

> ...Bathsheba ... gave birth to another son and named him Solomon. The LORD loved Solomon...
>
> **2 Samuel 12:24 (CEV)**

RESPOND
Think about how this passage makes you feel – angry, dismayed, confused? Can this be a spur to a longing for the final defeat of sin?

Bible in a year: Isaiah 31,32; Psalm 105

Family likeness

PREPARE

'O Lord, my Rock and my Redeemer, Gracious Saviour of my ruined life.'* Thank God for redemption that heals our damaged lives.

READ

2 Samuel 13:1–22

EXPLORE

We were warned of coming family breakdown (2 Samuel 12). Our own family's experience of fostering children taught us the sad lesson of generational dysfunctionality. All the children we fostered had a parent or parents who had been in care. Breaking that cycle is hugely difficult, although thankfully not impossible. David's lifestyle leaves an imprint on his family; their privilege breeding the sense of entitlement that says 'you take what you want'. His son Amnon is obsessed with his half-sister and his 'unprincipled self-indulgence'** leads to the intrigue that will end in Tamar's rape. Her resistance confirms there is no consent but his abuse of power, sadly modelled by his father, rides roughshod over all her objections.

The rape is quickly over and Amnon's desire turns to repulsion. But for Tamar, ejected as if she is the offender, the implications of abuse remain. She finds shelter in her brother Absalom's home, but is left 'bitter and desolate' (v 20, *The Message*), her whole life impacted by a moment of ultimately unsatisfying hedonism. Further trouble awaits as Absalom stores up his enmity. David is angry 'but he did not punish his son Amnon' (see verse 21).*** He loved Amnon for one thing, but he also was effectively silenced by the accusation of hypocrisy. What could he say? And so, a tragic episode begins.

Don't be misled – you cannot mock the justice of God. You will always harvest what you plant.
Galatians 6:7 (NLT)

RESPOND

Families desperately need our prayers. What are the needs of families around you? Is God calling you to help?

*'O Lord, My Rock and My Redeemer', Sovereign Grace Music, 2018. **Brueggeman, p287.
***The Dead Sea Scrolls manuscript and Greek Version add this phrase.

Bible in a year: Isaiah 33,34; Hebrews 2

Barren but not desolate

PREPARE
Repeat Psalm 63:3 a few times, allowing its truth to mould your thinking. Now turn to prayer.

READ
Psalm 63

EXPLORE

David is in the wilderness. At a time when wilderness experiences have become something of a trend, we need to think what that meant then. David is not there by choice on some retreat or thrill-seeking escapade. He is being harried, probably by his own son Absalom. He is cut off from his usual comforts without knowing when or whether this will end. This is compounded by trying to understand where God is in all this.

Self-absorption or self-pity might be my first port of call, but David's response is to look outward. The answers to his longing for security, sustenance and satisfaction are found in 'my God' (v 1). We see 'not the groping of a stranger feeling his way to God but the eagerness of a friend to be in touch with the one he holds dear.'* His thirst will not be quenched by anything else. He knows that from his past. He found satisfaction then, not in the luxuries of the palace or his kingly status but in God (vs 2,3,5). In his wilderness experiences of disturbed nights, he had turned his weary and troubled heart to God (v 6). By setting his heart on God he finds not just that he is clinging to God, but that God is holding him (v 8). And his 'but the king' (v 11) reference to himself speaks of hope. His time in the wilderness is not the final word.

Because your love is better than life, my lips will glorify you.

Psalm 63:3

RESPOND
What phrase from this psalm will remain with you?

*Derek Kidner, quoted in JA Motyer, *Psalms*, New Bible Commentary, 21st Century Edition. IVP, 1994.

Bible in a year: Isaiah 35,36; Hebrews 3

I'll be the judge of that

PREPARE

What do you deserve from God? Give thanks that we do not receive our just deserts.

READ

2 Samuel 13:23–39

EXPLORE

Tam's wife is a memorable character in Burns' poem Tam o' Shanter. What does she have in common with Absalom? Both 'nursed' their 'wrath to keep it warm'.* Tam's wife waits to give drunken Tam his due on his return. Absalom waits two years for the opportune moment to make Amnon pay for the rape of Tamar. His father David had done nothing. He would ensure justice was done. Shameful experience teaches us that justice for the sexually abused can be quietly ignored. But there are dangers in assuming we are to be the executors of judgement. Which is why Jesus issues his warning against arrogant judgementalism (Matthew 7:1).

Like his half-brother Amnon, Absalom is a skilled schemer but with bigger ambitions. Motivations for exercising judgement on others are almost invariably mixed. For Absalom there was anger and ambition behind his action.

He had one eye on the horrendous crime against Tamar, the other on the throne.

Absalom's haughty stance is apparent when he exhorts Amnon's assassins by echoing words spoken to Joshua on entering the promised land (Joshua 1:6,7,9). Confusing our human ambition with God's purpose and failing to recognise the seriousness of our sinfulness ('if I am guilty' (14:32) are a clear path to disaster.

'In your anger do not sin': do not let the sun go down while you are still angry...

Ephesians 4:26

RESPOND

Do you feel the criticism of judgementalism levelled at Christians is fair? How do we avoid assuming the role of judge that only God can play?

*Robert Burns, 1759–1796.

Bible in a year: Isaiah 37,38; Hebrews 4

Tuesday 20 September
2 Samuel 14:1–33

Who is in charge?

PREPARE

'God is working his purpose out as year succeeds to year.'* Reflect on this with thanks and reassurance.

READ

2 Samuel 14:1–33

EXPLORE

Three gifted but flawed characters move the story toward Absalom's rebellion. Joab is David's fixer, always a step ahead, anticipating the king's needs and getting things done. David is a great ruler, but his decision-making powers desert him in family matters. He struggles to handle Absalom and requires another parable (see 2 Samuel 12) to push him in the direction of partial reconciliation. Thirdly, there's Absalom, a determined, manipulative schemer who plays the long game. He burns Joab's barley as a statement that he will not be rebuffed. But notice the concentration on outward appearance that had caused Israel problems in the past. Saul's height and handsomeness (1 Samuel 9:2; 16:12) made him attractive, and Absalom's film star looks and celebrity family (vs 25–27) do similarly. But behind the prettiness lies a heart that has little awareness of humility (v 32).

This is a potent mix. The story plots the rise of Absalom, facilitated by Joab's desire to please, with David attempting to do the right thing. The conspiring to get David onside has much God-talk about it. But David's consent seems wrung out of him (v 21) rather than glad obedience. There is no perfect solution available. That's often the way in a messy world where God is at work even when all seems random.

Make your motions and cast your votes, but GOD has the final say.

Proverbs 16:33 (*The Message*)

RESPOND

'Did you think we would get through this without making any mistakes?' My realistic colleague's comment helped me gain perspective. Does it help you?

*'God Is Working His Purpose Out', Arthur Campbell Ainger, 1841–1919.

Bible in a year: Isaiah 39,40; Psalm 106

Making Israel great again

PREPARE
We are all leaders somewhere. But what kind of leader? Express your desires for your leadership to God.

READ
2 Samuel 15:1–37

EXPLORE
Even some of the world's worst leaders must be recognised for their patience and hard work. Their rise to power takes a slow, meandering path and a lot of palm greasing. Look at Absalom. 'In the course of time' (v 1), he begins to set out his stall, showing willingness to get up early and to listen to the unheard. Reading between the lines, David's administration was not coping adequately with the nation's needs. Absalom claims he is the answer. He will work for the people. A failure to take account of people's concerns can allow for the wrong sort of leader to gain traction.

Four years pass and now it's action time. Absalom has shown previously that he is not above a little deception to accomplish his purposes. He deceives both David and about 200 others invited to his feast. The *coup* becomes official, and the credibility of its threat causes David to flee Jerusalem. The episode provides clear contrasts. If deception, betrayal and self-confidence are hallmarks of Absalom, they sit alongside the dedicated faithfulness to David and the absence of hubris of Ittai (another outsider to Israel) and the true sorrow and trust in God that David displays (vs 25,26,30). These are the very things that mark him out as a man of God despite his manifest imperfections.

> Ittai answered, 'Your Majesty, just as surely as you and the LORD live, I will go where you go, no matter if it costs me my life.'
> **2 Samuel 15:21 (CEV)**

RESPOND
Having read this passage, what do you want to pray for leaders in society and the church?

Bible in a year: Isaiah 41,42; Hebrews 5

Leave it with me

PREPARE

Are you facing temptations to believe the worst about someone, defend yourself or claim your rights? How does the Lord want you to handle this?

READ

2 Samuel 16:1–23

EXPLORE

We're given a behind-the-scenes view of the opposing sides in the civil war. David's camp faces treachery linked to his predecessor, Saul. Absalom gives attention to how he can further humiliate David.

David was kind to Saul's grandson, Mephibosheth, treating him as family (chapter 9) rather than removing his head! But where is he now? Ziba, seizing an opportunity, lavishes gifts on David and reports that Mephibosheth is back in Jerusalem hoping for David's overthrow and the return to power of Saul's family. David impulsively disinherits Mephibosheth and Ziba benefits – see chapter 19 for the next instalment! David is then pelted with stones and cursed by the bold Shimei, another of Saul's relations.

David is anything but impulsive, which recalls Peter's description of Jesus who in the face of threats 'entrusted himself to him who judges justly' (1 Peter 2:23). Everything can be safely left in God's hands, even when our experience is tough and draining. Meantime, confusion is sown in Absalom's camp. The spy Hushai convinces Absalom of his loyalty but (plot spoiler) will eventually play a major role in ensuring his defeat. Ahithophel speaks with the authority of God, but his advice produces an act of bravado, tantamount to a war crime (v 22). As with many who oppose God, there is power to do evil, but victory will never be forthcoming.

'God opposes the proud but gives grace to the humble.'

1 Peter 5:5 (NLT)

RESPOND

Can you somehow follow the example of David's treatment of Mephibosheth and Shimei today?

Bible in a year: Isaiah 43,44; Hebrews 6

Sowing confusion

PREPARE
No weapons made to attack God's people can be successful (see Isaiah 54:17). Thank God for his restraining power and worship him as your protector.

READ
2 Samuel 17:1–29

EXPLORE
Chapters 13 to 19 make only occasional references to God's direct involvement. Sound logistics, military strategy and spread of misinformation are much more to the fore. But where God is acknowledged, his work is revealed as central to the narrative. Verse 14 makes this abundantly clear. God has 'determined to discredit' (*The Message*) Ahithophel's counsel and to bring ruin on Absalom. Otherwise, Ahithophel's proposed strategy of speedy, targeted action would likely have paid off. It's one of those 'what if?' moments beloved of some historians, turning history on its head. But there are no 'what ifs' when the restraining power of God is at work.

God accomplishes the downfall of Absalom by having the right people in the right place. David plants Hushai in Absalom's camp to counter Ahithophel's advice, presenting a plan that plays up David's military experience and emphasises the need to delay any pre-emptive strike. There follows a volte-face in which support surges for Hushai's plan. God's person is again present when Jonathan and Ahimaaz need to hide: a lady standing proudly in the line of Rahab as a protector of God's people (v 19ff). Finally, provision of food and drink is a sign not just of David's popularity but of God's enabling (vs 28,29). He is at work. To fight him ends in frustration, as Ahithophel's suicide ominously demonstrates.

'He thwarts the plans of the crafty, so that their hands achieve no success.'
Job 5:12

RESPOND
Knowing God makes us secure but not complacent, settled but not comfortable. Is this your experience?

Bible in a year: Isaiah 45,46; Psalm 107

Saturday 24 September
2 Samuel 18:1–33

Living with tension

PREPARE
'Behind a frowning providence, He hides a smiling face'.* Renew your trust in the promises of God, whatever your circumstances.

READ
2 Samuel 18:1–33

EXPLORE
David divided his troops into units, appointed commanders and began readying himself for the frontline. In an act of humility, he listens carefully to advice and remains at home (v 4). Not every leader responds so positively to such feedback. David had nurtured an attitude that knew when to say 'whatever seems best to you'. As preparations continue, we feel deep sympathy for David in the complexity of his double role. As a military commander, he looks for the rout that transpired. As a father, he commands that Absalom be treated with gentleness.

Joab, meantime, plays a key role at every stage of the story. He defeated the Ammonites, dealt with Uriah for David and arranged for Absalom's return. Now taking things into his own hands and disobeying orders, he shows anything but gentleness to Absalom. Joab is not troubled by complexity or hampered by the sensitivities of others.

Absalom is summarily executed (v 14). David is inconsolable. Even for God's anointed king, events seem to spiral out of control in this fallen world. We might wonder what part the promises of 2 Samuel 7:4–16 played in keeping him going in this turmoil.

Through these he has given us his very great and precious promises, so that through them you may participate in the divine nature, having escaped the corruption in the world caused by evil desires.

2 Peter 1:4

RESPOND
David probably felt overwhelmed. We all do at times. How can you help others who feel overwhelmed?

*'God Moves in a Mysterious Way', William Cowper, 1731–1800.

Bible in a year: Isaiah 47,48; Hebrews 7

Tables turned

PREPARE

Give thanks that Jesus speaks 'comfortable words'* to us, calling the weary to find rest.

. . . .

READ

Psalm 64

EXPLORE

Tell it like it is. That's what God wants us to do, not to pretend everything is OK. David makes a complaint to God, sharing his trouble about the way his enemies act with impunity and arrogance. They say whatever they like, hurtful and unjustified words that wound and scar (v 3). Social media is full of such uninhibited slanders, ambushing the unwary and causing untold damage. Are these not cause for taking our anger and perplexity to God in prayer? And every time we use words to tear down rather than build up, our sorrow needs to turn to repentance.

David complains, but as he works through his complaint it begins to dawn that he is not informing God of anything. There is no such thing as impunity in God's universe. Everyone is accountable and God will even allow people to cause their own downfall by their excesses (v 8; see also Romans 1:24–26).

The Book of Common Prayer (1928).

Eventually those who have put no control on their tongues will also have to acknowledge Jesus as Lord (v 9). David finally arrives at a perspective that will enable him to persevere even in the face of opposition. Being godly is not fruitless. It is the way of rejoicing and protection.

The righteous will rejoice in the LORD and take refuge in him; all the upright in heart will glory in him!
Psalm 64:10

RESPOND
The influence of social media on the way we speak about others is massive. It is the ultimate hiding place for ambushes. How can we be of most influence (with children and grandchildren, for example) in providing a different model?

. . . .

Bible in a year: Isaiah 49,50; Hebrews 8

Monday 26 September

2 Samuel 19:1–23

Post-war healing 1

PREPARE

Life's saddest moments involve loss through death and disagreement. Look with hope to that promised day which has no dying or tears (Revelation 21:4).

READ

2 Samuel 19:1–23

EXPLORE

A salutary lesson following cessation of war is that the aftermath can be as problematic as the conflict. Competing factions vie to fill the power vacuum, some look for reward and opportunity is taken to settle old scores. Chapter 19 largely revolves around these post-war challenges.

David's reaction to Absalom's death is vastly different from his previous bereavement (12:20). His deep personal grief threatens political stability (v 7). Joab steps in, exercising tough love to jolt David back into public leadership. Sometimes our pain can so turn us in on ourselves it makes us unconscious of needs outside our own and does not allow others room for celebration. David must address the genuine prospect of division amongst God's people (post-David and Solomon the nation will divide*). He needs to be welcomed back as king by those in both the north (Israel) and south (Judah) to maintain unity. How will he deal with those who opposed him? Shimei, a relative of Saul, had cursed David (16:5–14). Urged to take revenge, David offers forgiveness (vs 22,23), cementing his position by keeping Saul's descendants on side. We cannot but see in David something of what will be accomplished fully in the Lord Jesus, bringing unity in his family and forgiveness to rebels.

> He won over the hearts of the men of Judah so that they were all of one mind. They sent word to the king, 'Return, you and all your men.'
>
> **2 Samuel 19:14**

RESPOND

Pray for an end to conflicts around the world; for wise, gracious and unifying leaders.

*Read on through 1 and 2 Kings.

Bible in a year: Isaiah 51,52; Hebrews 9

Post-war healing 2

PREPARE
Thank God for the fellowship of faithful Christian friends.

READ
2 Samuel 19:24–43

EXPLORE
Absalom's death ends this attempt to overthrow David's kingship, but it is merely a lull before the next storm. In the brief respite, as David makes his return to Jerusalem, two men come to welcome him, Mephibosheth the grandson of Saul and the aged Barzillai.

David has his suspicions about Mephibosheth. He had been ratted on by Ziba back in chapter 16, accused of remaining in Jerusalem to side with Absalom against David. Mephibosheth's unkempt appearance suggested a different story; that he was more concerned about David than himself. And had David overlooked his physical disability? As a declaration of his commitment, he renounces all claims to his inheritance (vs 29,30). Mephibosheth of course had nothing but the kindness of David to rely on. It's a touching story of ongoing kindness and lasting gratitude. Barzillai is lauded for using his wealth to back David (v 32). But he looks for no personal reward other than returning to home comforts. His son, Kimham, will continue the family's faithful service. If we add to this the troops accompanying David (v 40), do we at last have a happy ending? Sadly, not. This is no fairy-tale. It's the record of sinful people in a broken world who bicker over status. No wonder Jesus calls us to be salt and light in this decaying and dark world.

'… I could expect only death from you … but instead you have honored me by allowing me to eat at your own table! …'
2 Samuel 19:28 (NLT)

RESPOND
Suspicion and resentment are destroyers of fellowship. Is there anything for us to put right there?

Bible in a year: Isaiah 53,54; Psalms 108,109

"I DON'T GO TO CHURCH BUT..."

95% of under-18s don't go to church. **BUT** many are open to faith.

Together we can reach them!

SCAN TO JOIN THE 95 CAMPAIGN FOR FREE

FIND OUT MORE AT THE95.ORG.UK

'Not with a bang but a whimper'

The title is taken from the final words of the poet TS Eliot's masterpiece, *The Hollow Men* (1925). Eliot's weary conclusion about the world's end could also be used of the main character in this series of readings. King David is nearing the end of his life and we sense that he is now a broken man. His political and military victories are distant memories. The man who united warring tribes and established a kingdom is now a shadow of his former self.

His daughter Tamar is raped by her half-brother Amnon (2 Samuel 13:1–21), who in turn is then murdered by another one of his sons, Absalom (2 Samuel 13:23–39). Absalom plots a coup d'état against David and comes to a brutal end (2 Samuel 18:9–15). Much of David's history does not make for easy reading, and without giving the game away, this series of readings will feel uncomfortable to our modern western sensibilities.

Themes of revenge and bloodshed abound (chapters 20 and 21), sitting uneasily alongside wonderful songs of praise (chapters 22; 23:1–7). The series ends on an ambivalent note, as David courts the Lord's displeasure by carrying out a national census (chapter 24:10). But despite his many failures, Israel remembered him as their greatest king and Jesus himself was hailed as a Son of David (eg Matthew 15:22).

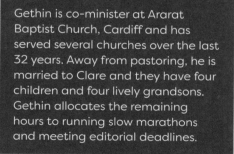

About the writer
Gethin Russell-Jones

Gethin is co-minister at Ararat Baptist Church, Cardiff and has served several churches over the last 32 years. Away from pastoring, he is married to Clare and they have four children and four lively grandsons. Gethin allocates the remaining hours to running slow marathons and meeting editorial deadlines.

Yesterday's man

PREPARE

In an age of catchphrases and soundbites, I come before the creator of heaven and earth, the maker of things seen and unseen. The one who knows my waking and sleeping. Before him, I still my heart in simple trust.

READ

2 Samuel 20:1–26

EXPLORE

'All political careers end in failure' is a remark attributed to Enoch Powell, a once controversial MP. This could be applied to King David in these last few chapters of 2 Samuel.

After the exhaustion and pain of Absalom's defeat, David is now dangerously vulnerable to more attacks. His past glory will not help him now. Sheba, son of Bikri, smells this weakness and makes his move. He is a populist leader, appealing to the tribal loyalties of Israel, stirring up loathing against the establishment based in Judah and Jerusalem. And he's an effective leader; all the men of Israel desert David and go with him.

There's something strangely familiar about this storyline. Separated, as we are, by thousands of years and a culture that's barely recognisable, this drama has a contemporary feel. A weakened power base, an opposition that appeals to strong national emotion and the lure of a civil war. This sequence of events has been repeated across all cultures and across history.

> Now a troublemaker named Sheba ... happened to be there. He sounded the trumpet and shouted, 'We have no share in David, no part in Jesse's son! Every man to his tent, Israel!'
>
> **2 Samuel 20:1**

RESPOND

'I remember all those whom I know who are under pressure and feel like giving up. Lord, I ask that you give them streams of living water.'

Bible in a year: Isaiah 55,56; Hebrews 10

A mother's love

PREPARE

Lord, I would live today in the knowledge of your great love and care. Injustice and cruelty are all around, but I ask that you help me go deep into your love and show this to everyone I meet.

READ

2 Samuel 21:1–14

EXPLORE

This is not an easy story to read or apply. David's prayerful response to a famine results in God directing him to an historic massacre conducted by his predecessor Saul, who pursued a policy of executing a number of Gibeonites, even though they were protected by an historic oath (Joshua 9).

This injustice is avenged by the execution of seven of Saul's sons, bringing the famine to an end. But within this bloodthirsty tale, we encounter the mother of two of the executed men sitting on the rock where they are displayed. The dead men are not given a proper burial, their bodies exposed to the elements. Rizpah sits and mourns until the rains come and the famine ends.

There's dignity here in the midst of revenge and loss; a mother whose only desire is to give her children a decent burial. For the sake of her loved ones, she faces down the bitterness of her enemies and guards their remains. There are times when circumstances render us speechless and all we can do is love and wait.

After that, God answered prayer on behalf of the land.

2 Samuel 21:14b

RESPOND

'Lord, I pray for those whom you have given to me to love and nurture. I commit them to you and your loving care.'

Bible in a year: Isaiah 57,58; Hebrews 11

A haunting song

PREPARE

In the ordinariness of my life and the simplicity of this moment I come to you. You are my rock, my fortress and my deliverer. I open myself to you, Father, Son and Holy Spirit and pledge myself afresh to you.

READ

2 Samuel 22:1–16

EXPLORE

This song of praise has quite a history in David's life. Its setting in this chapter suggests that these are his final words (see 23:1). But this is the work of a young man.

With only a few variations, we are in Psalm 18, ascribed to David as he sang to the Lord when the Lord delivered him from the hand of all his enemies and from the hand of Saul. This incident is chronicled in 1 Samuel 31 and 2 Samuel 1 but it may also have been written during the period leading to David's enthronement (2 Samuel 2–5). It's a long psalm of extravagant praise and imagination.

Once David's cry is heard in God's temple, there are earthquakes, fire, smoke and drama as the Lord acts on his behalf. So why does this psalm crop up again at the end of his life?

Maybe David regarded this psalm as his signature tune. Maybe this poem encapsulated the deep song in his heart. Maybe we too have a signature tune that speaks of God's dealings with us.

In my distress I called to the LORD; I called out to my God. From his temple he heard my voice; my cry came to his ears.

2 Samuel 22:7

RESPOND

What are the words, images and experiences that have shaped my spiritual life? Can I speak them out to God or turn them into a piece of writing or music?

Bible in a year: Isaiah 59,60; Psalms 110,111

Subscribe to *Daily Bread* for just £16* annually

Take out or renew your subscription in three easy ways:

Online: su.org.uk/bible-guides **By phone:** 01908 856000 **By post:** Complete this form and send it to **Freepost SU MAIL ORDER**

* Reduced cost for payments made by Direct Debit – saving you both time and money

---

Subscribe by post (please complete both sides of this form)

I want to take out an annual subscription to *Daily Bread* ✔

You will receive the next quarter's guide (October–December 2022 edition), and your annual subscription will renew on the date of first subscription. You can cancel at any time.

Title: [   ]   Full name: [   ]

Full address: [   ]

[   ] Postcode: [   ]

Tell us if you don't wish to receive postal updates:

We will send you updates about the difference you are making to children and young people's lives through your giving, and offer you further opportunities to ensure the good news is shared. However, if you would rather not receive such information, please tick here [ ]

Tel. No. (Home): [   ]   Mobile No. [   ]

Email address: [   ]

Email contact: Please keep me updated on the latest resources from Scripture Union, please tick here [ ]

Scripture Union will never sell your data or share it with another company or charity for marketing purposes. You can change the way we contact you at any time by contacting Scripture Union: 01908 856000, via our website or emailing hello@scriptureunion.org.uk. You can read our full privacy policy at: www.su.org.uk/privacy

---

Could you top up your subscription with a donation?

At Scripture Union, as well as producing Bible reading guides, we create opportunities for children and young people to explore the Bible and respond to Jesus. Your subscription is already helping to fund this vital work but through a top-up donation, you could help make even more impact. It's estimated that 95% of all under 18s in England and Wales don't go to church. Your gift could help us take the good news to even more of them!

A top-up gift of £4 could subsidise a child or young person's place at an SU camp
A top-up gift of £9 could gift children in a primary school class a children's Bible
A top-up gift of £20 could help an SU worker set up a new youth club in a deprived area

Add £4 ◼   **Add £9** ◼   **Add £15** ◼   **Add £20** ◼   Add £ [   ]

Payment

If you choose to pay by Direct Debit, your subscription will cost just **£16**. If you prefer to pay by cheque or card, the cost for the year is **£19**. If you are able to top up your subscription with a donation, your gift will reoccur annually along with your subscription (unless you let us know otherwise). Thank you.
Note: *This form is for UK subscriptions only. For overseas subscriptions, see su.org.uk/bible-guides*

Please fill in the relevant section below based on your preferred method of payment:

Bank details

Instruction to your Bank or Building Society to pay by Direct Debit.

NAME & FULL POSTAL ADDRESS OF YOUR BANK OR BUILDING SOCIETY

To: The Manager Bank / Building Society Name:

Full address:

Postcode:

Name(s) of Account Holder(s):

Bank or Building Society Account Number:

Bank Sort Code:

Service User Number (SUN): 8 4 0 6 5 1

Reference number: (for office use)

Instruction to Your Bank or Building Society
Please pay Scripture Union Direct Debits from the account detailed in this instruction subject to the safeguards assured by the Direct Debit Guarantee. I understand that this Instruction may remain with Scripture Union and, if so, details will be passed electronically to my Bank or Building Society.

Signature(s):

Date: D D M M Y Y

Note: Banks and Building Societies may not accept Direct Debits instructions for some types of accounts.

Pay for your subscription by cheque or card payment

Subscription cost £19   Optional top up donation £   Total cost £

Cheque payable to Scripture Union ☐ WRITE YOUR CHEQUE NUMBER HERE   Postal order ☐

Please debit my credit/debit card ☐

Card no:

Issue no/valid from: ☐☐ / ☐☐   Expiry date: ☐☐ / ☐☐   Security no:

Card holder's Signature:

Date: D D M M Y Y